Symbology of the Temple of the Sagrada Família

Symbology of the Temple of the Sagrada Família

Text by **Albert Fargas** | Photographs by **Pere Vivas**

Gaudí engraved on a block of stone of the Temple the ground plan of the Sacristy, in the tradition of the old master builders of cathedrals.

The numbers in red show the position in the architectural setting of the Temple

Introduction

The work of Antoni Gaudí falls within the artistic current called Modernism. It was a movement indebted to Romanticism and had its roots directly in pre-Raphaelite and symbolist styles. The basic traits of Modernism are the exuberance of forms, the ornamentation, the attention to detail, the use of plant motifs, the preference for curves and asymmetrical lines, the dynamism of the forms, etc. Gaudí, however, was a unique architect, the author of an unrepeatable oeuvre; an oeuvre that was marked by the construction of the Sagrada Família, a work he built simultaneously for many years alongside the construction of other emblematic buildings. Nevertheless, the final years of his life were dedicated body and soul "to the construction of the temple", to the construction of the Expiatory Temple of the Sagrada Família.

"On making this temple I set myself the idea of following one of our traditions, a tradition that fits us perfectly, the Mediterranean tradition. All architectural style has emerged from the shelter of the temple, and all new art that that comes should be the same."

Antoni Gaudí

Architecture by Gaudí

The architecture of Antoni Gaudí possesses many aspects and has many faces. In relation to the context of this book, however, I wanted to highlight just one: the symbolic content. Gaudí himself said, "I am geometry, which means synthetic". We should remember that the Greek etymology of symbol (*sim-bolon*) means "that which joins". In this sense, symbolism is something that is synthetic yet inductive. Therefore, to the statement that he was geometry and synthetic, Gaudí could have added that he was also symbolic.

The symbol is a consubstantial part of Gaudian architecture, it is an intrinsic

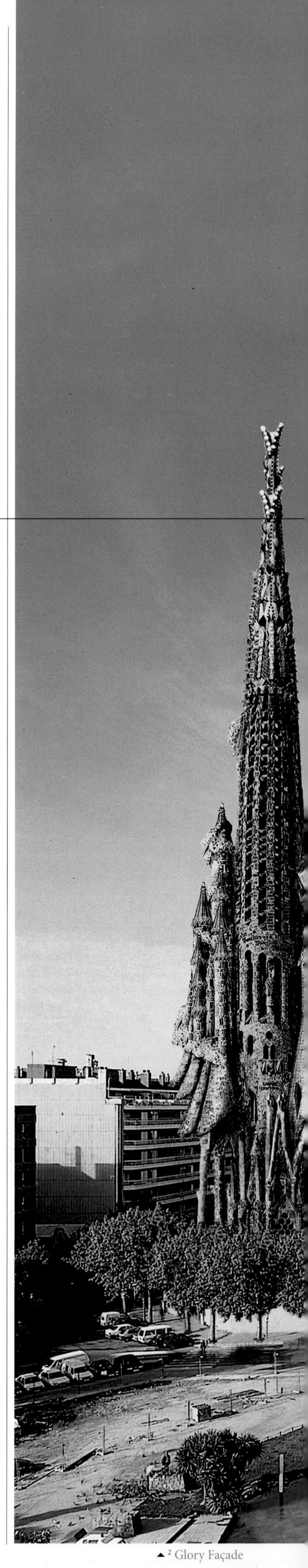

Photomontage that shows the appearance the temple will have according to Gaudí's project.

▲ 2 Glory Façade

▲ 1 Nativity Façade

▲ The apse (page 40)

and fundamental aspect of the forms and volumes of his works. This aspect, present in all of Gaudí's architecture, in the Temple of the Sagrada Família takes on a special precision: it is at the service of the Catholic doctrine. The Sagrada Família, as the cathedral it is, becomes a catechism of stone, in "a book written in stone". It is also a homage to the creator and an extension of the great book of creation or nature, written by God. This, however, would be another aspect of Gaudí's architecture.

The symbolism of the Sagrada Família is obviously framed within the Catholic doctrine and liturgy; it could not be any other way.

Nevertheless, the Sagrada Família is something more than a catechism of stone. The remark by Fulcanelli about cathedrals fits perfectly with the idea that Gaudí had of the Sagrada Família: "The cathedral, sanctuary of tradition, science and art, should not be seen as a work solely dedicated to the glory of Christianity, but rather as a vast realisation of ideas, tendencies, popular beliefs, a perfect whole that we can go to, without fear, every time we have the need to think more deeply about our ancestors in all the spheres: religious, secular, philosophical or social".

Antoni Gaudí's attitude is the same as that as the man from traditional societies, in which all activity had a sacred reference. The construction of the temple imitates the creation of the world. The same occurs, however, with all the trades and arts, since the human being has been placed on earth *ut operator*, "to work in it", in other words, to continue with the divine creation. It is therefore perfectly logical that Gaudí said that, "The history of architecture is the history of the temple".

Statue of King Solomon in the chapel of the Rosary.

The temple

Every temple is a cosmic image of the universe for two reasons, because the activity of the constructors reproduces in ritual form the creative activity of God —it is a recreation of the world—, and because it must be built following the rules that Jehovah revealed. Consequently, the construction of a temple must always follow the divine model and instruction.

Gaudí faced the construction of the Sagrada Família following the most authentic Judeo-Christian tradition, which places the origin of all temples in the Temple of Solomon. The importance of this temple obviously lies in its nature of divine revelation. God, through the sacred texts, gives specific instructions about the building that should house the Arc of the Covenant. According to tradition, the plans for the construction of the Temple of Jerusalem, or of King Solomon, were revealed by God to Solomon's father, King David.

If the Expiatory Temple of the Sagrada Família is a temple built to the Glory of God, it must be directly inspired by his hand, and his constructors, with his architect at the head, are just —although no small thing— instruments of divine action. It could not be any other way. Everything, absolutely all the building (ground plan, measurements, symbols, etc.) must refer to this homage and subordination to the divine will.

The history of the temple in western architecture is therefore linked to the diverse interpretations of biblical writings. In this sense, one of the concerns if the constructors of cathedrals —of which Gaudí is, without doubt, a continuing force— will consist of discerning which stylistic order most suits the divine revelation.

Besides religious or ideological considerations, for an architect there can be no greater professional challenge than the construction of a large temple. The explanation for Gaudí's exclusive and almost obsessive dedication to the Sagrada Família, in my opinion, lies in this, and more so when some of his contemporaries argued that he was aware of producing the great temple of Christianity. His contribution to the controversy of the constructors of cathedrals about which style best suited the divine revelation is the abandoning of the biblical writings and the desire to read directly the texts of nature, understood as a reflection of divinity. In this way, the dispute about the architectural styles would be overcome.

Francesc Pujols said: "The vision of the Sagrada Família is worthy of being compared to the Vedic visions of India, the Homeric visions of Greece and the Gothic visions of medieval Europe, which filled our continent with cathedrals".

The temple is by definition a reflection of the divine world, a piece of heaven on earth, or also a meeting point between heaven and earth. Or, said another way, the house of God on earth. As Saint Maximus the Confessor wrote, "it is worthy of admiration that, being so small [the temple], it is similar to the grandness of the world..." In this sense we can say that it is a branch of heaven on earth or an attempt to move a part of the world beyond to the world down here below. Etymologically, *templum* is the sector or sample of heaven that the Roman auguries studied to make predictions, and by extension came to designate the space or building in which the observation was made.

"The Great Architect of the Universe", lamina of a French bible from the 13th century.

Nature as a model

All temples must imitate nature, because all temples are, according to tradition, "cosmic". In other words, it is made imitating the world, imitating nature, inasmuch as it is a work of God. The temple is an image of nature, because nature is the work of God and the temple is a sacred space built by men to praise God. We can therefore say that the temple-nature is the original temple, because it was obviously "built" before the Temple of Jerusalem or Temple of Solomon. Along the same lines, all the temples built throughout history are the same temple. All are a single temple, because they are a replica of the divine order or macro-cosmos. They are the imitation of the same model: nature.

Consequently, the Gaudian attitude of imitating nature in his architectural work is fully coherent with his religious fervour. Since for a believer the human being has been placed on earth to continue the divine work.

Gaudí, however, went much further than the Modernist movement in the sphere of architecture, because Modernism imitated natural forms only as decoration, whereas he studied the constructive laws of nature to solve architectural problems. Gaudí never made a literal imitation of nature, but rather approached that which he considered the essence of natural forms, since it was not about copying nature, but harmoniously building, following its laws. This is because the temple should not aim to be a "realistic" image of the world, but rather a "structural" one; in other words, it must produce the intimate and mathematical structure of the world. It must seek out and imitate the harmony of this world.

The temple built by men must be an imitation —in the sense of prolongation or continuity— of the grand temple that is nature, which is the work of God, of the beginning or of the grand architect of the universe. "The great book, always open and always a good idea to make the effort to read, is that of nature; other books have come out of that and also have the interpretations and errors of man. There are two revelations: one, doctrinaire, of morals and religion; and the other, a guide through the facts, which is that of the great book of nature" (*Imitating the work of nature*). With the project of the Sagrada Família we can say that Gaudí united or reunited both revelations. This is why it is said that the symbols of the Sagrada Família are related to one of the two revelations, or form part of Christian iconography or nature. In any case, these two sources are ultimately related, in that one derives from the other. A text by Philo of Alexandria explains it clearly: "The supreme and true temple of God is the cosmos as a whole. As a sanctuary it has the holiest part of the reality of the universe; heaven; as sacred objects, the stars, as priests, the angels". Every part of the temple corresponds to a part of the cosmos. When the sacred forests become houses or buildings, the rudimentary enclosures become walls, the trees pillars, stone is the altar, the cave becomes the shrine of the apse and the roof is assimilated into heaven, etc. It can be said that the temple is a sacred landscape petrified or worked in stone.

Gaudí's architectural attitude, however, is not only motivated by his religiousness of Christian faith: there are intrinsically architectural reasons, a long way from its religious nature. "Architecture creates the organism and that is why it must have a law in consonance with nature", said the architect. Even more so, "everything comes from the great book of nature; all the styles (architectural) are organisms related to nature".

Nature is the organism of organisms, in which we find all the structures, all the architectural solutions. It is therefore the only model to be taken into account. It is what he baptised with the name of "geometry of nature". Just like all products of pharmacopoeia come from products we find in nature, all

Pinnacles of the Temple compared with stalks of *Sedum nicaeensis*, the forms of which, it seems, inspired Gaudí.

Spiral staircase of one of the towers of the Nativity façade and longitudinal section of the shell of a horned auger (*Turritella communis*)

TATO

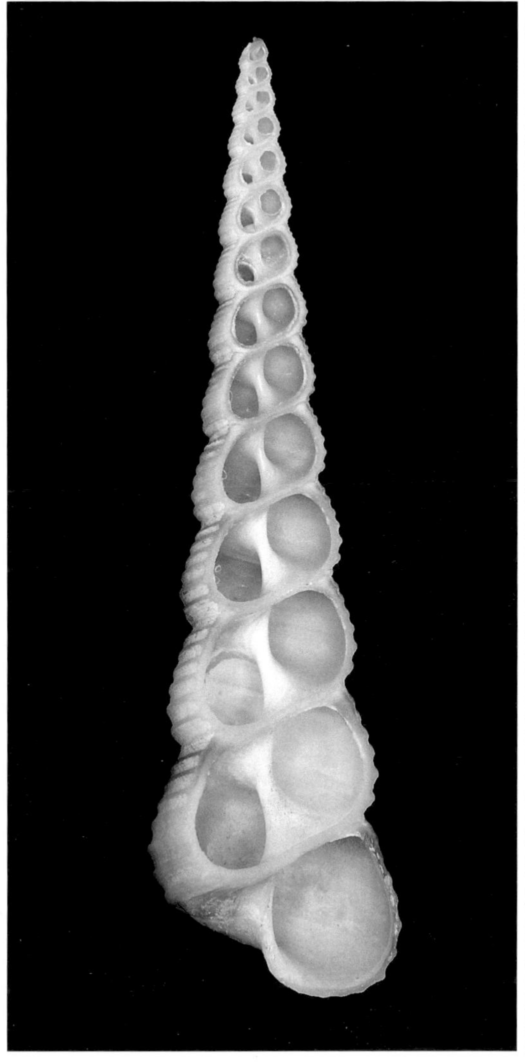

architectural organism of structure comes from the organisms or structures of nature.

Looking for solutions in creation, Gaudí incorporated the plant structure, animal movement and the geometry of mineral crystallisations into architecture, in other words, the essence of creation.

As a result, Gaudí's architectural attitude could only be that of imitating the divine work: nature. It would have been strange if it had been any other way. It is, then, a case of profound coherence, and he emphasises it with the answer he gives when asked who his teacher is and he says his teacher is the tree he sees through the windows in the courtyard of the workshop. For Antoni Gaudí, the first and main book of architecture was nature.

The stones of all temples must be a continuation, a new chapter in this book. In the sense of the Gospel of Luke: "I tell you that, if these [the disciples] should hold their peace, the stones would immediately cry out".

The interior of the crypt of the church of the Colonia Güell is similar to the small wood that surrounds it.

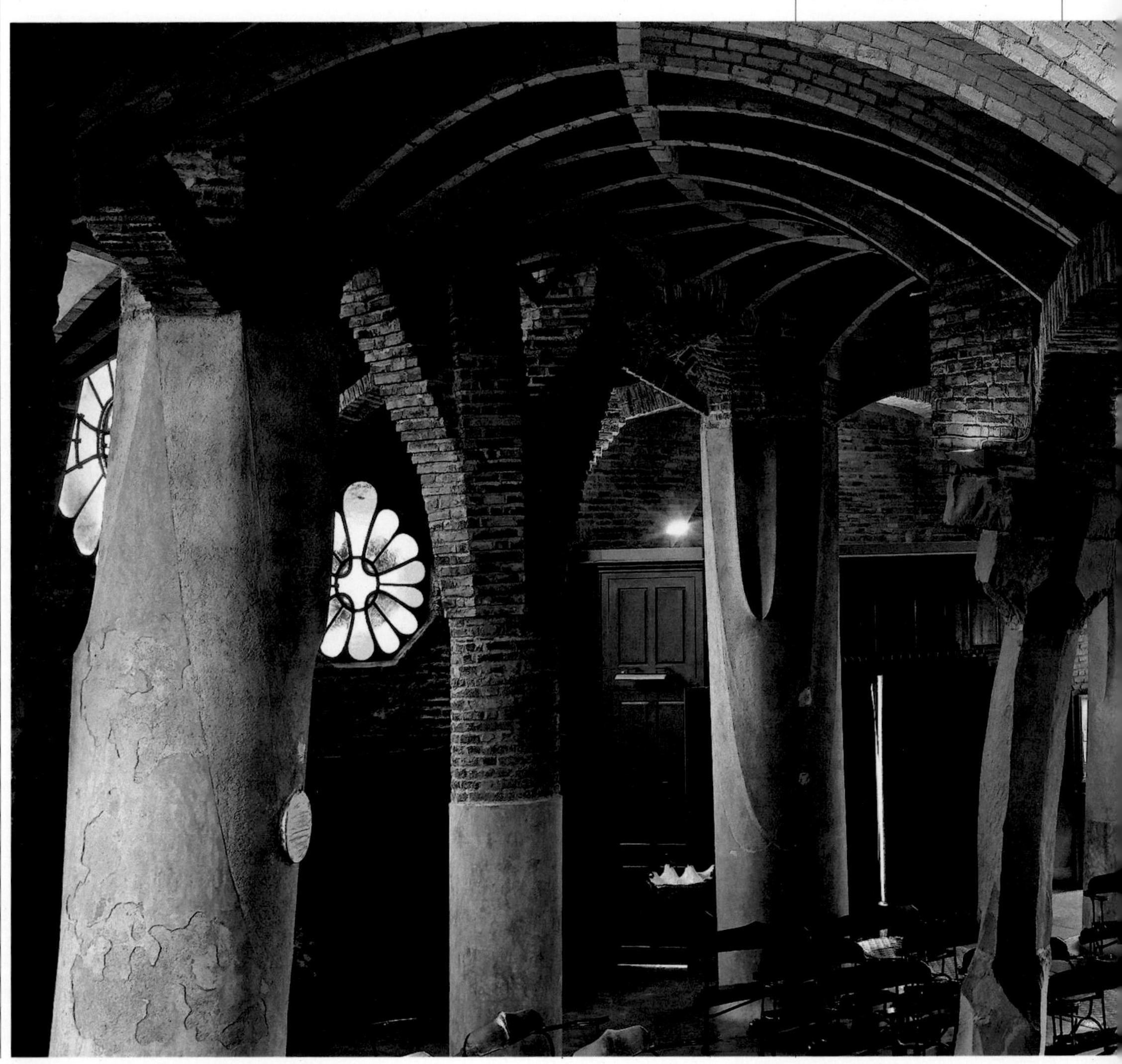

Sacred symbols

We can say that the Sagrada Família is sacred art and not religious art. The difference between the two is more than of nuance. There is an abyss. Sacred art is a prolongation of the incarnation, of the act of divine creation, and religious art is not. Sacred art must reveal the trace of what is divine in creation. Therefore, it is clearly logical that it is inspired by nature, in the divine creation, which is a creation or recreation of the great work. Because all the creatures of the sensitive world lead to God: they are the shadow, the trace or the image of the beginning of all things.

In a way of artistic expression understood in this way, the artist or creator cannot just leave it to inspiration. When he works, he must not express his personality. He must seek in nature a perfect form that responds to the sacred models of celestial inspiration.

Sacred art must be symbolic because it must translate into images the correspondence between the unmanifest and manifest world. Heaven must come down to earth. Or it must go from 1 to 2. This is the function of sacred art, which must never be confused with religious art. Moreover, in sacred art nothing is gratuitous or the result of pure fantasy, everything has its raison d'être, its explanation.

The silhouette or skyline of the Sagrada Família fully participates in the symbolism of the temple-mountain. The parallel nature of the symbolism of the temple with that of the mountain occurs because both represent the

Massif of Montserrat.

mystical centre or meeting point between the two worlds, between heaven and earth. In the mountain the realisation of this symbol is the peak, and in the temple, the altar. The peak brings us closer to the world above, heaven. In this sense, both the temple and the mountain are central points of the world or stairways that enable us to rise and bring ourselves closer to the world of the spirit. The outline of the Sagrada Família, which recalls the outline of a mountain, with the corresponding peaks and summits, strengthens this symbolic synonymy between temple and mountain, just as occurred with the Babylonian and Egyptian temples, the Ziggurats and the Pyramids; or with the Gothic cathedrals.

The poet Verdaguer understood it immediately on tracing a parallel nature between the forms of the mountain of Montserrat and the characteristic towers of the Sagrada Família.

Mont Saint-Michel, example of temple-mountain.

Symbolism of the Sagrada Família

The symbolism that Gaudí reflects in the Sagrada Família is not sustained only through the imagery and the painting, but also incorporates the symbols into the architecture, giving an expressive character to his works. This is one of the most significant characteristics of all Gaudian architecture. This is why some commentators have classified the Sagrada Família as a mystical poem.

On the same line, it can be said that Gaudí's architecture in the Sagrada Família is the mysticism represented by the sensuality of natural forms, or what is the same thing, the morphology of nature.

The old dichotomy between functionality and beauty of the symbol is nearly always brilliantly solved in Gaudí's work. To the false question as to what should prevail, the catechistic intentionality or the expressive beauty —a variant of the classical polemic between background and form— Gaudí's reply is always based on the great divine guide: nature; where, incidentally, this dichotomy is not posed, because it has no sense. The adoption of this attitude relates Gaudí to traditional thought, which does not conceive a form separate from a background. The external is always a reflection of the internal. In short, two levels manifest the same reality. Therefore, they can never be seen separately, as two different things.

The inspiration in nature was so intense and evident that for the production of the sculptures he used life-size models emptied with plaster: human

The Devesa in Girona and tree-like structure of the central nave of the Temple of the Sagrada Família.

beings —living or dead—, plants, diverse objects. If the result was not what he expected, he had mannequins built, on the other hand easier to manipulate than human beings. The sculptures, therefore, like his architecture, are based on the structure of the forms.

The forms or the geometry can act on nature, on the reality of the setting and, above all else, on people. When the form of a building is added to the materials —clay, wood, stone, etc.—, which at the same time has its particular energy, we obtain an authentic "creation" as a result. This is why buildings have life, and therefore their own energy. Without doubt, we find structures and forms with the capacity to provoke emotion and spiritual heightening. Temples, such as the Sagrada Família, must invite contemplation and serenity.

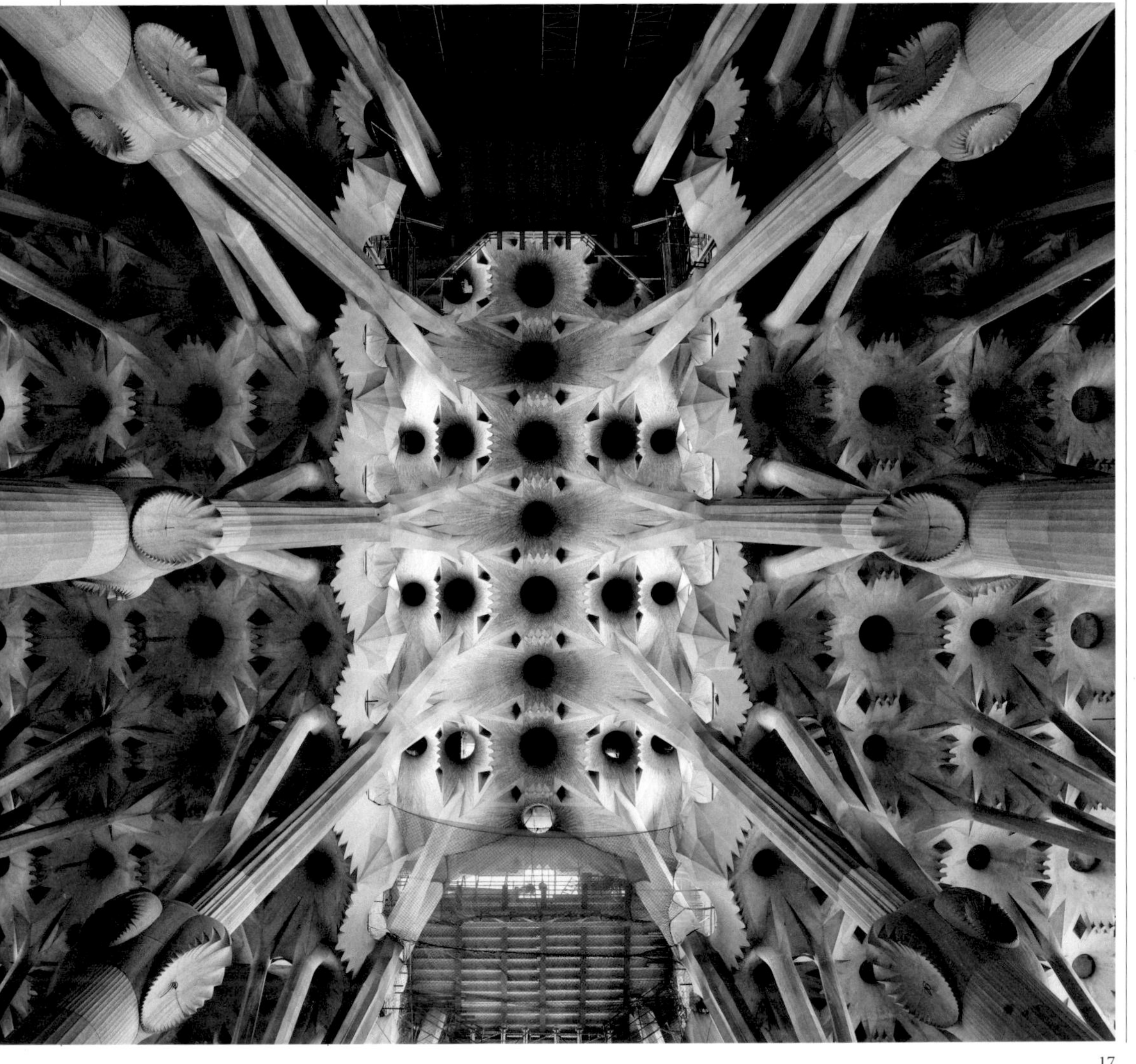

Expiatory Temple of the Sagrada Família

"Everyone finds their own things in the temple. Peasants see the hens and cocks; scientists the signs of the zodiac; theologians the genealogy of Jesus; but the explanation, the reasoning, is only known by the competent and should not be popularised."
Antoni Gaudí

Expiatory Temple of the Sagrada Família

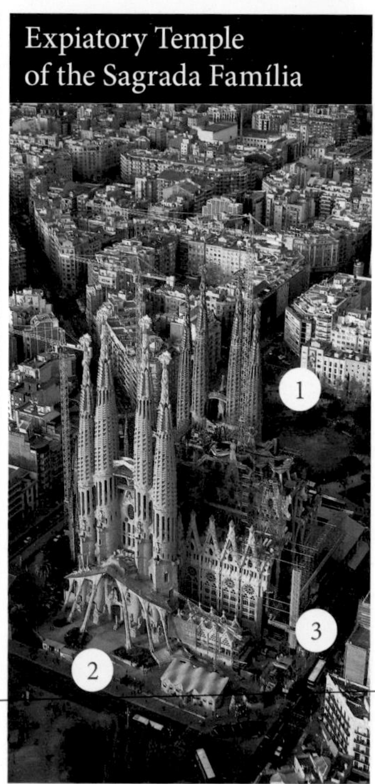

1-3 The façades
The ground plan
The interior of the Temple
The cloister and the four obelisks
The apse
The sacristies
The exterior walls
The bell towers and domes, the spiral staircases and the bells
The crypt

1-3 The façades

In a temple the façade must provide a synthetic vision of what it houses inside. it has been said that the façade of a temple is the equivalent of a person's face, that is, the mirror image or reflection of what we can find inside.

Using journalistic terminology, we can say that the façade is the front page of the newspaper, on which we can read the headlines for the news we find inside the paper or inside the temple.

In temples, the form of the façade is usually related to a clear vertical axis that associates it with the image of the heavenly mountain. In my opinion, the representation of this heavenly mountain in the Sagrada Família, with the three façades and 18 towers, surpasses in this sense many Gothic cathedrals, since not only the façade symbolises the mountain but the entire volume as a whole evokes the idea of mountain. The design of three doorways per façade, with the higher central one, strengthens this symbolism.

Historically, the façades of cathedrals have also had the function of enlightening the faithful who could not read. The statues, frescos, etc. formed the great illustrated book that the people read. The façades of

Eixample district of Barcelona.

CARRER ARAGÓ
CARRER PROVENÇA
AVINGUDA GAUDÍ
1
PLAÇA GAUDÍ
CARRER MARINA
3
CARRER SARDENYA
2
PLAÇA DE LA SAGRADA FAMÍLIA
CARRER MALLORCA
AVINGUDA DIAGONAL
PASSEIG DE SANT JOAN

cathedrals and temples have been, even before Gothic style, the Bible of the poor. With those of the Sagrada Família Gaudí recovers this function.

However, the knowledge provided through the symbols —like those of the façades of cathedrals— is not only intellectual and rational, but is also existential and dramatic knowledge, which appeals to intuitive and direct knowledge. The recognition of a symbol, as its very etymology shows, is an act of reunion or re-encounter between two aspects of the same reality, the two sides of the coin, which when joined together fit perfectly. In the symbolic act, a part of the coin is the physical symbol, and the other is the bearer of all that is human. When these two parts are joined and fitted together, we obtain the coin. A symbolic act is carried out.

Furthermore, the natural place where there must be sacred symbols is the temple. This is because the ritual or liturgy is the dramatisation of the symbols we find on the façades or the interior of the temple. Obviously, moreover, the natural place or space of the liturgy is the temple.

The two arms of the cross of the Sagrada Família correspond to two façades, the east one, facing northeast, and the west one, facing southwest. The east façade is that of the Nativity —Carrer Marina—, and the west façade, that of the Passion and Death —Carrer Sardenya—. At the base of the Latin cross is the main façade. That of the Glory —Carrer Mallorca—, facing southeast. On the northeast facing part of the temple the apse is placed —Carrer Provença.

This arrangement of the façades is not gratuitous, since the life of Jesus Christ that is explained on these three façades follows the movement of the sun. The Nativity Façade receives the first rays of sunlight. That of the Glory or plenitude of Jesus Christ is the main façade, facing south, and that of the Passion and Death correspond to the west, where the sun ends its daily cycle. With this arrangement, the daily movement of the sun corresponds to the life cycle of Jesus Christ and the sun-god of many pre-Christian religions corresponds to the Christian God. If Gaudí had been at the head of the work from the very beginning, this correspondence would have been perfect and harmonic —the Nativity Façade to the east, that of the Passion and Death to the west and that of the Glory to the south, in the middle of the day—, but when Antoni Gaudí took over the work, the orientation of the building was already determined by the crypt, built by his predecessor, the architect Francesc de Paula del Villar.

Drawing of the Sagrada Família by Antoni Gaudí in 1902.

The ground plan

Although, as we have just seen, Antoni Gaudí did not design the ground plan of the Sagrada Família following the traditional method, among other reasons because it was his predecessor on the project who began the works on the crypt, we should look at this method for dealing with the ground plan of the temple.

The foundations of the temple are oriented with a gnomon that enables us to draw the two axes (*cardo*, north-south, and *decumanus*, east-west). It is a practically universal method, present in all sacred architecture, and was used in Europe until the end of the medieval era. In the centre of the site chosen a gnomon is placed, and around it a large circle is drawn and the shadow cast by the gnomon is observed; the maximum space of separation between the morning and afternoon shadow shows us the east-west axis, and two circles centred on the cardinal points of the former show, by the intersection, the angles of the square. We can say that this operation is the squaring of the solar circle.

The synthesis or summary of all sacred architecture, and of the temple in particular, is the "squaring of the circle" or transformation of the circle into the square. The founding act of the building starts with the orientation to the east, since this is the ritual that relates the cosmic order with the worldly order. The cosmic order is the circle and the worldly order is the square. When a temple is built, the cosmic order drops to the earth and the square is transformed into a circle.

It is interesting to recall the three basic operations in the founding of a temple: marking the circumference, marking the cardinal axes to orient the building and marking the square of the base. This is because these three operations correspond to the three fundamental symbols of the temple: the circle, the cross and the square.

The ground plan of the Temple of the Sagrada Família is a basilica building of five naves with transept of three, which form a Latin cross. The two arms of the transept correspond to the Nativity and the Passion and Death façades. It follows the organisation of Christian cathedrals, which in the macrocosmos-microcosmos relation reproduce the latter, a hanging human figure; God made man, Jesus Christ nailed to the cross. The apse corresponds to the head, the cross-aisle or transept the two arms, the nave represents the body and the altar is the heart.

The ground plan in the form of Latin cross of the Sagrada Família, and of the vast majority of Gothic cathedrals, is in debt to the neo-Gothic model advocated by Viollet-le-Duc. The Gaudian contributions, however, such as the forest of columns, the parabolic vaulting, the dizzying heights and others, cast off all historicist rigidity.

On the other hand, the form of the ground plan presents a clear coinciding with the symbolism of the cross, prior to the crucifixion of Jesus Christ. The words cross and crucible have the same root, which symbolises what is in the alchemical crucible where the primary matter, Jesus Christ, experiences the Passion; it is in the transept-crucible where Jesus Christ as primary matter must die in order to be able to be resurrected, purified, spiritualised and transformed, which, on the other hand, is what is done in the ritual of the Eucharist.

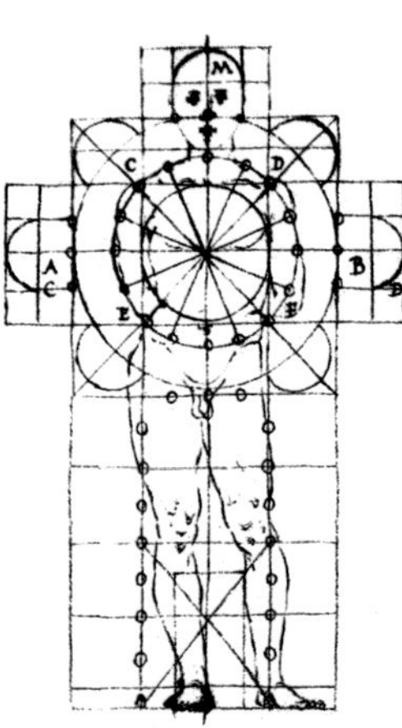

The ground plan of Christian cathedrals is a Latin cross or a human figure with the arms extended. Drawing by Francesco Giorgio, 1460-1540.

Ground plan of the temple. Drawing by Francesc Berenguer.

Design of the ground plan of all holy temples from the shadow that the sun projects in the central circle.

ASSUMPTA
SAGRISTIA
SAGRISTIA
VESPRES
MAGNIFICAT
JESUCRIST
MARE DE DEU
ESPERIT SANT
GLORIA IN EXCELSIS
JOAN
LLUC
JESUCRIST
TE DEUM LAUDAMUS
MATEU
MARC
PASSIO
NAIXEMENT
CAPACITAT = 5.550
OCEANIA
BAPTISME
PENITENCIA
ANDREU
PERE
PAU
JAUME
LA CREACIO
OFICIS DE L'AIGUA
LA CREACIO
OFICIS DEL FOC
PARE ETERN
ESPERIT SANT
JESU-CRIST
MARE DE DEU
S. JOSEP
ADAM EVA
C. DE
MALLORCA
GLORIA
BROLLADOR
AIGUA
TEIERA
FOC
PRIMAVERA
TARDOR
PLANTES DE

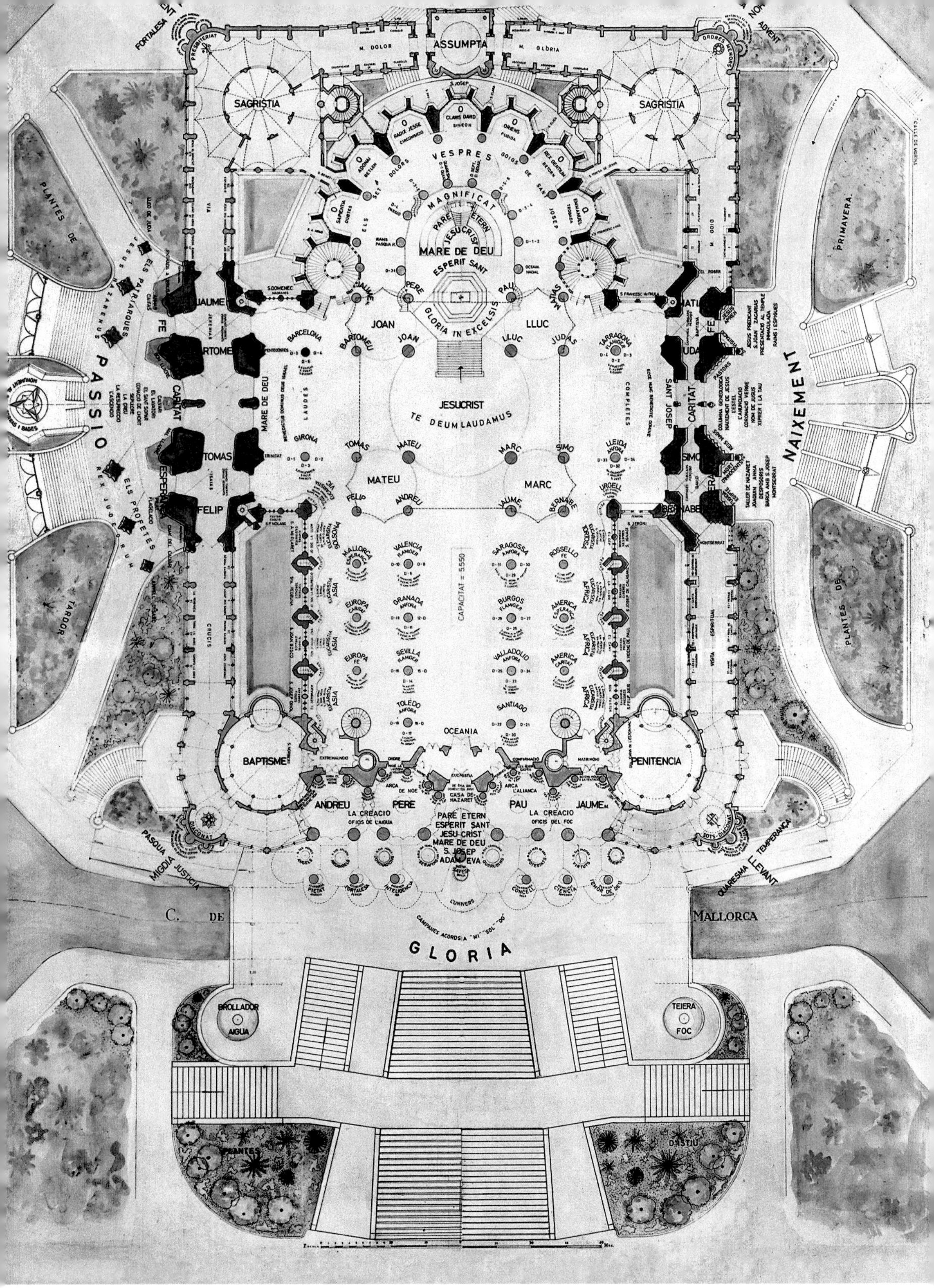

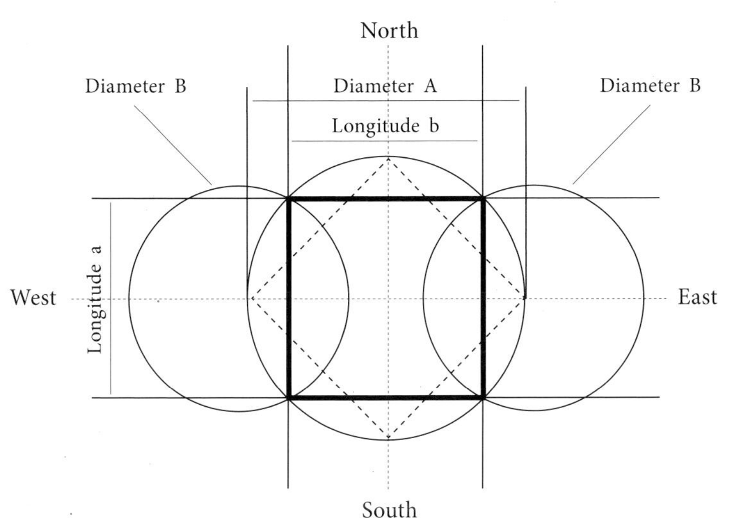

North
Diameter B
Diameter A
Diameter B
Longitude b
Longitude a
West
East
South

The interior of the temple

As Gaudí said, "the interior of the temple will be like a forest". That is how it will be, because the orientation and organisation of the columns recall the trees of a forest. The pillars of the main nave will be palm trees; they are the trees of glory, sacrifice and martyrdom. Those of the side naves will be laurels, trees of glory, of intelligence.

It is also planned for the light to create a state of semi-darkness that strengthens the sensation of being in a leafy forest, an aspect that will be further strengthened by the decoration of plant structures, a recreation that recovers the Celtic idea of the forest as a temple par excellence, where the Druids held ritual ceremonies. This idea harmonises perfectly with that of Gaudí of continuing the divine work through the construction of a temple, taking into account that the great model and prototype temple of other temples is nature.

The elements in the interior of the temple will aim to create an atmosphere of profound religiousness that favours mystical ecstasy. The chromatic projection through the light, the forms, the dimensions, etc., will be focused in this direction. This is, on the other hand, the essential function of all temples, to create a sacred atmosphere or space, an alternative to the profane space, in which the space-time coordinates of the "normal" world are altered and modified, since all temples are a part of heaven on earth.

The altar will receive all the light from the large windows in the dome, which will also light up the central space, the large transept of 30 x 40 metres. The dome is the exaltation of the temple. It has an exterior and interior life, must provide light to the altar, since the transept is the darkest place in the temple and over it must be placed the crowning of the building to accentuate its pyramidal form.

The Gospel will be present though fragments of the Sunday mass, represented by figures of the characters that intervene in the evangelical description —as if they were paintings of a strip cartoon with rhyming couplets— on the ledges of the triforiums alongside the columns of the central nave, so that they can be easily contemplated by the faithful when they are listening to mass. We would say that they are audiovisual reminders that illustrate the Sunday Gospel. The epistles will also be present, but in the form of texts and situated in the knots or capitals of the columns, under the representation of the evangelists. The dominical letters will be arranged according to the cycle of the liturgical year, two per column. The first dominical letter of the Advent will begin in the north column, the closest inside to the Nativity Façade, and will continue from right to left —anti-clockwise— towards the apse, where the columns of Nativity, Septuagesima, Lent and Easter are. The central nave and the interior side of the transept will house the dominical letters of the Pentecost.

The four daily prayers or canonical hours —matins, lauds, vispers and complines—, which are the basis of the liturgy, will also be present in the interior of the temple, with their final hymns as a means summary. Of the matins, the *Miserere* will be written on the handrail of the lateral choir galleries, and the *Te Deum laudamus*, beneath the dome, in the triforium at the height of the relieving arches of the central nave. The lauds will be represented by the canticle of Zacharias *Benedictus Dominus Deus Israel,* in the gallery of the transept wall. The vispers will be in the apse, with the hymn of the Virgin, the *Magnificat*,

Interior of the Temple. Drawing by Francesc Berenguer.

(Pages 26-29)
General view of the interior of the Temple. The tree-like columns and starred polygons of the vaulting recall the interior of a wood.

SANTIAGO
VISIO DEL PRESBI

written on the railing of the triforium that closes at the level of those of the central nave. The complines, with the canticle of Simeon *Nunc dimitis*, on the railing of the chapel of the Virgin, on the other wall of the transept.

With the names of the saints inscribed on the columns, the interior liturgical representation will be completed: the hours, days and times —that is the hymns—, the calendar of saints' days and the dominical letters, because the saints are the cornerstones or ashlar of the Church.

The four columns of the transept will be dedicated to the four Evangelists and will be decorated only with their symbols. The twelve columns surrounding this transept, outlining a circle, will be dedicated to the twelve apostles. The two that will support the triumphal arch, and which will therefore be situated on either side of the altar, will be dedicated to Saint Paul and Saint Peter. The position of the other ten, dedicated to the other apostles, will correspond to those of the bell towers of the exterior façades. In this sense, in the Temple of the Sagrada Família there will be a correspondence between the internal and the external, between the esoteric or interior and the exoteric or exterior. This correspondence is exact and precise on the Nativity and Passion façades, while on the Glory Façade the columns of Saint Peter and Saint Paul will be placed as the two entrance columns to the temple that show the threshold between the profane world and the sacred world. They are the columns of the Sun and the Moon from the Temple of Jerusalem or the J and B columns of a Masonic temple, realisations of the cosmic duality. In the Temple of the Sagrada Família the columns of the main entrance to the temple of the Glory Façade sum up the duality through the apostles Peter and Paul. In this case it is a double threshold, first in the entrance to the temple and after when the columns of Saint Peter and Saint Paul support the entrance arch to the altar, to the *sancta santorum* of the temple.

The arrangement in circumference of the twelve columns of the twelve apostles tells us of the cosmological models; in other words, the explanation of the world. It is the organisation of reality in the form of circumference, the symbol of the totality divided into 12 parts: the hours of a clock, the 12 astrological signs, and others.

The remaining columns will be dedicated to the bishops, the continuers of the apostolic work. Those of Catalonia (Tarragona, Vic, Lleida, La Seu d'Urgell, Girona, Solsona, Tortosa, etc.) will be the columns of the transept. Those of Spain (València, Granada, Santiago de Compostela, Toledo, etc.), the columns of the central nave. On the side columns and interior pillars of the façades we will find the remaining bishops of the world, thus signifying the ecumenical nature of the Catholic Church.

The form planned by Gaudí to dedicate columns to a diocese will consist of placing the patron saints of these with quotes taken from the prayers of their saints' day, with the respective guardian angels. The saints will rise up the columns in a spiral and the angels will descend from the vaulting along the columns. The spiral forms are infinite, rise up, without limits, like eternity; it is like the spiritual life of the souls that contemplate God, infinite Being. This is what the columns of the Sagrada Família will be like. We will have grouped together the saints and the guardian angels, by diocese. As Gaudí himself said, the interior symbolism of the temple will be based on the balancing point between the saints that rise from the earth to heaven and the angels who drop from heaven to the earth. All temples must be the meeting point between the two main planes of reality, the world here below and the world up above. The Sagrada Família, the Holy Family, however, will not only be in the columns of the naves, but is a concept present throughout the temple. For example, in the dome of the apse will be represented the Eternal Father and on the folds of his clothing will appear heads of seraphs. From the highest triforium of the apse

Current view of the ambulatory of the Temple apse.

will hang a lantern of seven wicks as a symbol of the seven gifts and fruits of the Holy Spirit.

The architectural solution adopted by Gaudí to represent the Holy Trinity is extraordinary. The vaulting, hyperbolic paraboloids generated by a straight section which is moved over another two on a different plane, are a magnificent symbol of the Holy Trinity, because they are two straight, infinite generating lines, and a third, also straight and infinite, which is supported over the other two: the Father and the Son, related by the Holy Spirit; the father and the Son are the directrixes and the Holy Spirit, the generatrix. The three are equally infinite and are one single thing. As a symbol of the Holy Trinity it is better than the tree with three branches, because this suggests breaking off from the trunk.

Hanging in the triumphal arch, extended from the column of Saint Paul to that of Saint Peter, the baldachin will be the heaven of the altar. It will be crowned by a cross, at the foot of which will emerge a grapevine that will be trained with bunches of grapes. Gaudí would often say: "¿Do you want something prettier than a table placed beneath a trained vine?", referring to the altar. Around the baldachin will hang a chandelier of fifty lamps that will represent the Holy Spirit, to symbolise that the Father and the Son send the Holy Spirit to the Church.

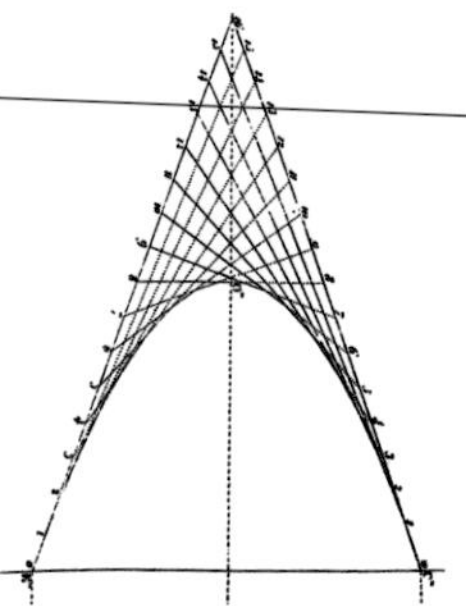

Hyperbolic paraboloid, symbol of Gaudí of the Holy Trinity.

On the triforiums of the transept of the Nativity Façade will be Saint Joseph, surrounded by angels who will be offering him the tools of his trade. On the triforiums of the Passion Façade will be the Virgin surrounded by angels, with the attributes of the litany. The crucifix of the high altar will complete the representation of the Holy Family (Saint Joseph, the Virgin and Baby Jesus), dedication of the temple.

On the vaulting there will be angelic figurations, anagrams of Jesus, Mary and Joseph, the names of Christ with the sceptre, tiara and sword and diverse symbols, such as the sign of infinity.

In each connection of four columns that support the lateral naves there will be an amphora and burner, alternating, on the line of the central nave; and on the divisions of the two lateral ones, the symbols of Jesus Christ with references to faith, hope and charity. The first will be represented by a tau over the boat of the Church, with the keys of Saint Peter, the bread and the wine; an amphora with a five-pointed star adorned with alpha and omega, over the Ark of the Covenant, will be the symbol of hope, while a cross enhanced by four rivers over walls will symbolise charity.

As we have said, all the interior of the temple will symbolise the action of heaven over the earth. The peace and life of celestial Jerusalem, where the house has the lamb that symbolises the light that guides the faithful. This action is focalised on the altar, where the light of the temple and the meaning of the images will converge, because it is the spot where every day the transmutation of the Eucharist, passion and death of Jesus Christ occurs: the mass.

Among other elements, the twelve fruits of the Holy Spirit will be symbolised by some horns of plenty. The columns will also symbolise the tree of life that grows on both sides of the square. On the central vaulting, the branches and leaves of this tree will be the palm, symbol of the glory and triumph of martyrdom. In contrast, on the lateral naves there will laurel leaves, symbol of the Glory of intelligence. In the middle of these leaves one will be able to see birds from the earth.

Another element important for their use and symbolism are the railings. There will be representations of all the hierarchies of angels on the vaulting and on the nine railings of the triforiums and choir galleries of the dome, apses and naves, which will represent the nine angelic hierarchies. They will

Statue of Saint George, work of Josep M. Subirachs, that overlooks the central nave.

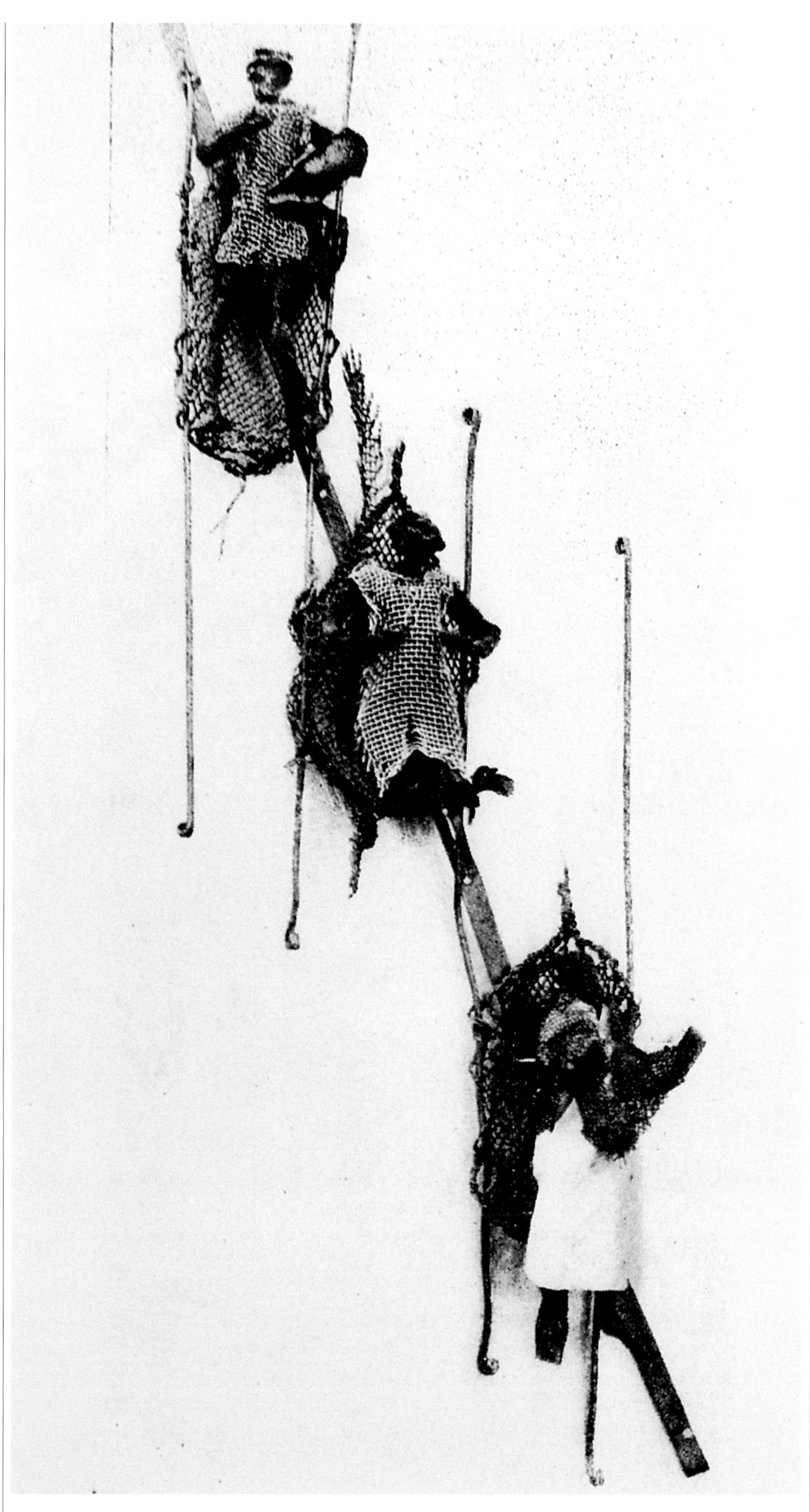

Photographs of the models made by Gaudí of the angels of the central nave of the Temple.

shine out like the angels; all will be angelic figures according to the visions of the prophets and of the Apocalypse, angels with six wings.

In each of the large elliptical windows of the lateral naves one will see the figure, vigorously coloured, of Jesus Christ of the parables. The transparency of the glass and the colours, with lights positioned behind, will light up the temple at night with diverse colours, an effect that the stained-glass windows will complete, which will allow the diffuse sunlight to pass through, while they will receive the light from the other elements. This play of lights and colours through the large windows will symbolise that the saints receive light or strength through Jesus Christ.

Finally, on the interior projecting passage, a little way up the side walls, some mosaic fishes will swim towards the high altar with their mouths open and others will return from the altar with the Sacred Host in their mouths after taking communion. This mosaic will receive the light from the other elements, which will be reflected throughout the temple; like the works of men when they are inspired by God.

According to this arrangement, the angels of the railings will have their own light, since they are spirits created since the beginning. The saints will receive illumination through the figure of the Jesus Christ of the stained-glass windows and they will extend it throughout interior of the temple. The cleric of the mosaics will receive the light of the angels and saints and will be spread around the temple, following the example of the saints.

(Right and next page) Knots or capitals of the columns inside the Temple that show their ramification.

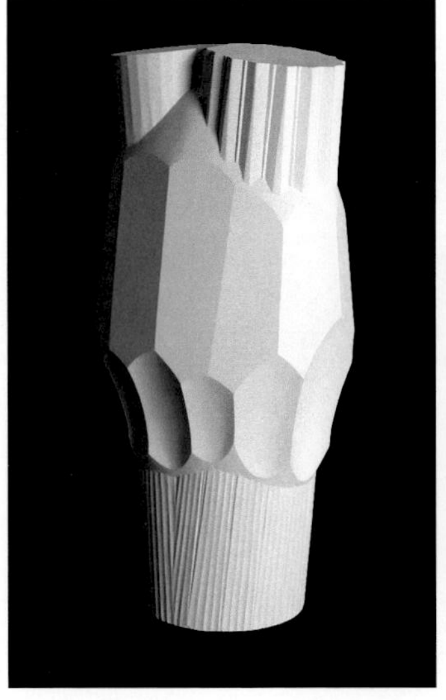

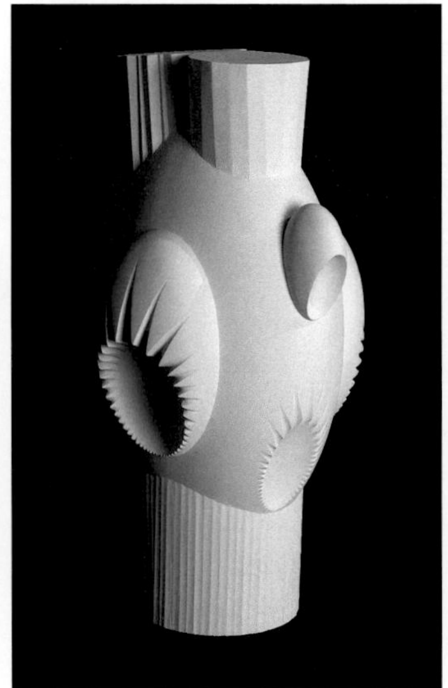

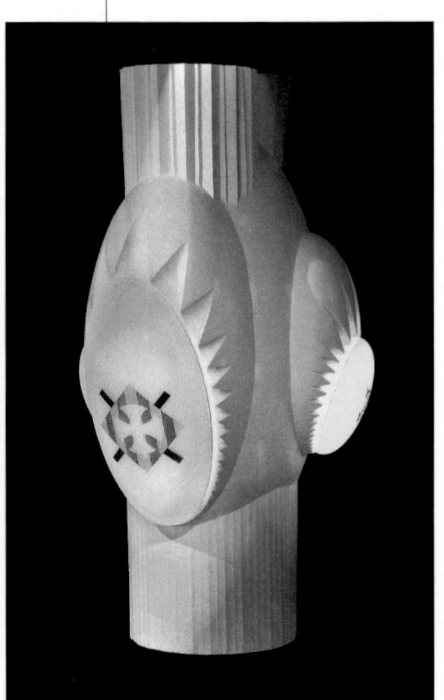

Diverse types of knots of the tree-like columns of the interior of the Temple; the third model shows how the electric lighting will be once fitted.

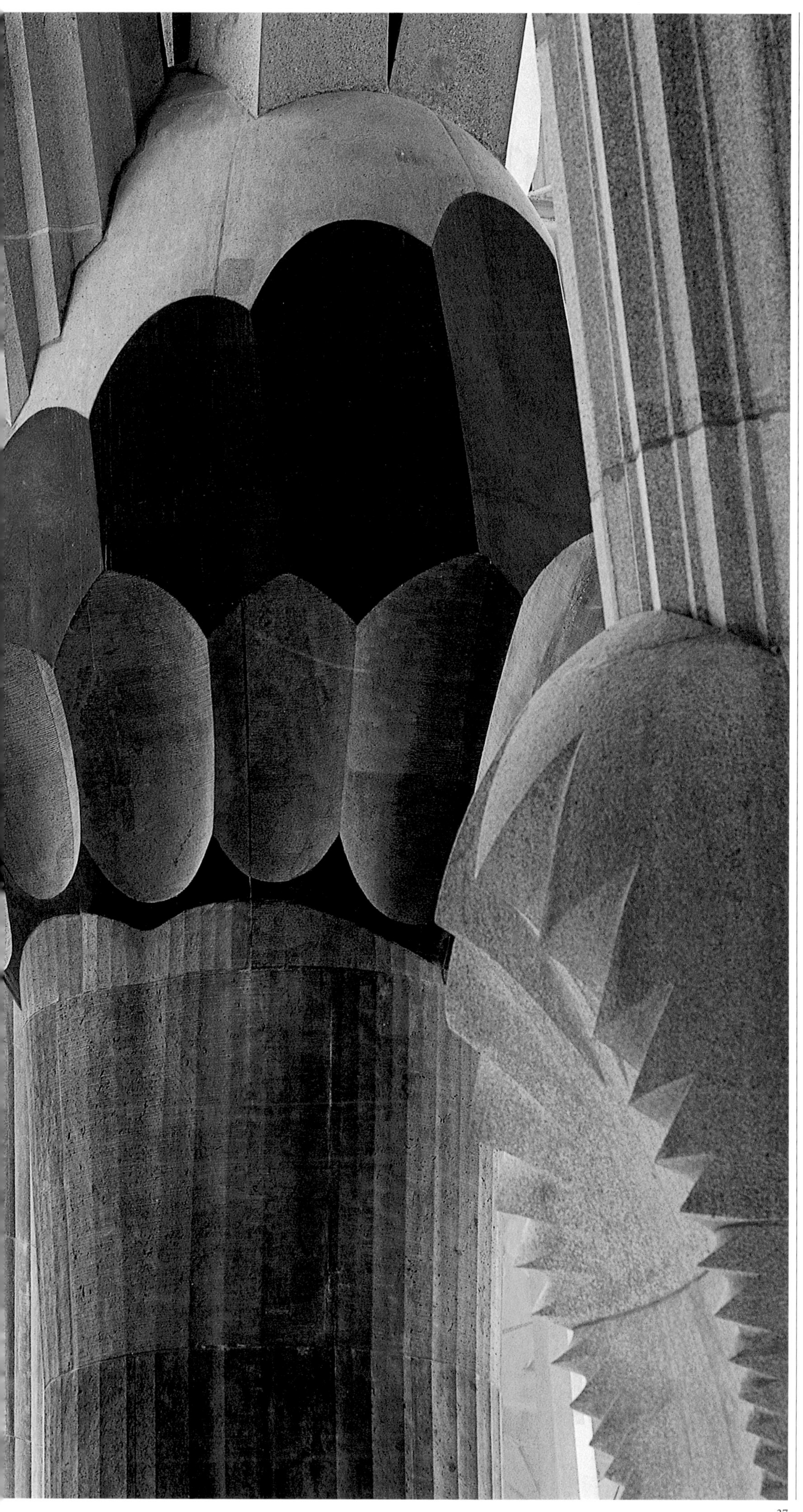

The cloister

A cloister is a sacred city, a celestial Jerusalem. It is the crossing point of the four directions of space, of the four points of the compass. A well or tree situated in the very centre of the cloister often indicates the *omphalos* or centre of the cosmos.

The arrangement of the cloister of the Sagrada Família is totally original and unique. It does not include the atrium, as in Latin basilicas, and neither is it situated to one side of the church, as in medieval cathedrals. In the Sagrada Família it surrounds the temple, closing it off within a rectangle, like a moat that separates the sacred space from the profane space. The centre of the cosmos of the cloister of the Sagrada Família is the temple.

The cloister also has the function of communication or distribution between the diverse rooms and is an ideal space for processions to move through. The fact that it is the meeting point of the four directions favours this use. Gaudí had said: "The cloister will be made to pray the Rosary in procession and to insulate the temple from the noise of the street". On the pinnacle of the first pediment we find the symbolic anagram of the Holy Family: a cross, a saw and an M.

Each intersection of the cloister with a façade leads to an ornamented door, in dedication to the Virgin Mary. The two of the Nativity Façade are dedicated to the Virgin of Montserrat and that of the Rosary (the only one built). On the Passion Façade the doors are dedicated to the Virgin of the Mercè and that of the Dolores.

A cloister is the meeting point between the three levels of the universe: the underground world or sub-world, the earthly world and the heavenly world. Each one of these has its symbol, present in the majority of cloisters. The well represents the sub-world, the surface is the earthly world, and the tree, the rose bush or column symbolise the heavenly or divine world. The majority of cloisters possess these three elements.

The cloister is, however, above all else, the centre of the world, because the centre of the world is the point of union and communication between heaven and earth. The square or rectangular form of the cloisters, as an open space below the heavenly vaulting, emphasises their function as intermediary between heaven and earth. The cloister is, in short, a symbol of intimacy with divinity.

The arrangement of the cloister of the Sagrada Família, surrounding the temple, emphasises its symbolic functionality: a space of union between the interior of the temple or spiritual world and the exterior or profane world.

(Right page)
Ornamented door dedicated to the Virgin of the Rosary situated on the intersection of the cloister with the Nativity Façade.

Pinnacle of the first pediment of the cloister with the anagram of the Sagrada Família: beneath the cross of Jesus, the saw of Saint Joseph with the M of Mary intertwined.

Pediments of the outer walls of the cloister.

(Right page)
Photograph of the apse and drawing by Francesc Berenguer of what it will be like.

The apse

Dedicated to the Virgin, an admirable example of fertile virginity. The concept of the fertility of the virgins extends to the founding saints of religious orders: Saint Anthony the Abbot, Saint Benedict, Saint Scholastica, Saint Bruno, Saint Francis of Assisi, Saint Clare and Saint Elias. The seven chapels, in the form of a half hexagon, are dedicated to these saints, whose images are situated in the buttresses, base and canopy. The pinnacle of the canopy ends with the anagram of Christ, while that of the buttress culminates in cereal ear. The seven chapels will also recall the seven sorrows of Saint Joseph and in each one there will be a Holy Family.

On the high railings of the chapels, around the lanterns, is the floral ornamentation mentioned in the antiphony of the *Little Office of the Blessed Virgin Mary*: the cedar, symbol of immortality; palm trees, resurrection and immortality; the cypress, eternal life; the cinnamon or tree of paradise; roses, perfection and revival; the olive tree, which symbolises peace and serenity, and balsam, oleoresin. Symbolically, all these floral elements are synonyms, since from different angles their symbolism refers to immortality and eternal life.

The ears, whether from cereals or from the most humble plants that flower all over, crown the ends of the pediments and pinnacles. Fleeing from these Marian symbols, in the direction of the earth, are the reptiles that take the form of gargoyles, snakes, dragons, salamanders and lizards.

The lanterns of the seven chapels, pyramids of an octagonal base, culminate with invocations to the Messiah, symbolised by the antiphonies of the last week of Advent, called the O. The symbols are placed within a large O and are: *O Sapientia, O Adonai, O Radix Jesse, O Clavis David, O Oriens, O Rex gentium* and *O Emmanuel rex* [Puig Boada, p. 54] (10·03).

The two sets of stairways that border the apse on both sides are crowned by ears. Here stand out the gargoyles, sea snails with a large outline beside the eastern *Levante* and land snails beside the western *Poniente*, and some lower channels supported by perforated corbels.

Plaster model of the chapel of the Assumption situated in the middle point of the apse.

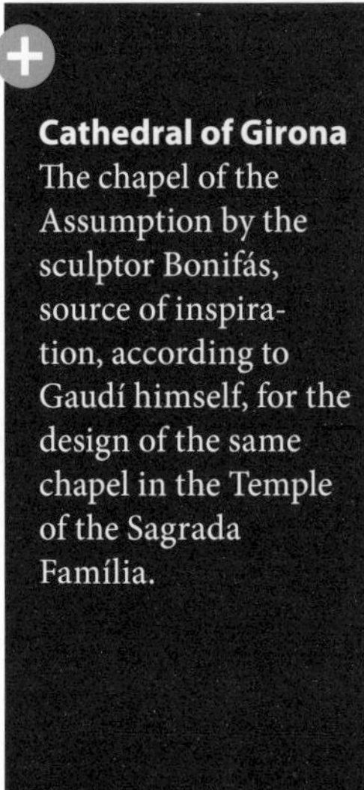

Cathedral of Girona
The chapel of the Assumption by the sculptor Bonifás, source of inspiration, according to Gaudí himself, for the design of the same chapel in the Temple of the Sagrada Família.

Sanctus Sanctus
Sanctus

Pinnacles inspired by plant motifs of the apse.

Gargoyles with animal motifs of the apse.

The Baptistery and the Chapel of the Penitence

The Baptistery and the Chapel of the Penitence will flank the Glory Façade, corresponding to the seven doors that represent the seven sacraments, the first of which is the sacrament of the Baptism and the last that of the Penance.

The early Christian baptisteries were mostly given an octagonal ground plan. The fountains or baptismal fonts took on, by extension, this form.

The importance of the octagon lies in that it is the intermediate geometric form between the square, the symbol of the material world, and the dome, symbol of the celestial world. Architecturally, the dome or spiritual world cannot rest directly over the square ground plan and constitutes the building of the cosmic model. The square base must be turned into an octagon so that it can support the circular dome.

This function of intermediary between the material world or square and the spiritual world or circle is one that affords value to the octagonal figure. It is the squaring of the circle.

We also find hexagonally-shaped baptisteries. In these cases, emphasis is made on another aspect of the baptism, that of the burial of the fallen or of sin, which links the Penance with the Baptism. The former represents the death of sin and rebirth of a new life, the Baptism being like a cosmic penitence that pardons the original sin of humanity.

In this sense, the ritual of the baptism has as an original gesture the total immersion in water, since according to Saint Paul it is the immersion in death with Christ and of the resurrection of new life. The current ritual of baptism, the anointing of water on the head, vaguely recalls this profound original symbolism, which links this rite of initiation, which at the end of the day is the sacrament of baptism, with that of other initiation rites, such as that of the mysteries of Eleusis, the freemason.

The baptismal fonts were placed on the outside of the temple, before entering, with the aim of reproducing the impossibility of the non-baptised entering into church, or what amounts the same, that to form part of the Church, first one had to be baptised. Thus, the symbol was experienced in a traditional way and therefore fully, since when the joining of the Church was represented, it was both in the church as building and the Church as community or communion. For this reason, the baptismal fonts are situated at the entrance of the churches or in a chapel apart. Consistent with the sense of initiation and regeneration of the baptism, Gaudí places the chapel of the Baptism just by the entrance of the main façade and in its own space.

The symbolism of the baptistery is also related to that of the holy water stoup. Every time one of the faithful enters the temple and crosses themselves, with the fingers previously wetted in the stoup, they are reproducing the sacrament of the baptism. With the holy water the purification of the baptism is repeated.

Chapel of the Penitence, drawing by Francesc Berenguer.

Sanctus
Sanctus
Jesus
Maria Josep
35.41

The four obelisks

The four obelisks of the four corner buildings of the cloister are a pattern of the temple and correspond to the four cardinal points, which at the same time are related to the four cardinal virtues and the Ember Days or Seasons. The Ember Days are old penitential liturgical celebrations that consist of three days fasting during a week at the beginning of the four seasons. In the past they took place in the first week of Lent and Whitsun, the third week of September and the third week of Advent. The four obelisks are:

(*a*) South (Baptistery), the intersection between the Glory and Passion façades. It is the summer (Season of Whitsun) and the symbol of Jesus is a sun with a cross. In relation to the cardinal virtues —to each cardinal point corresponds a cardinal virtue— it is justice, with the usual representation of the scales and the sword.

(*b*) West (Sacristy), intersection between the Passion Façade and that of the apse. It is the autumn (Season of September) and the symbol of Jesus is the anagram. As regards the cardinal virtues it is strength, symbolised by a helmet and a cuirass.

(*c*) North (Sacristy), intersection between the façade of the apse and the Nativity Façade. It is the winter (Season of Advent) and the symbol of Jesus is the name Emmanuel. In relation to the cardinal virtues it is prudence, represented by a snake and a chest.

(*d*) East (Chapel of the Penitence), intersection between the Nativity and Glory façades. It is the spring (Season of Lent), the central obelisk culminates in a cross and the INRI. In relation to the cardinal virtues it is temperance, symbolised by a knife that cuts bread and a *porrón*, the typical drinking jar with a narrow spout. According to Gaudí, "thanks to the *porrón*, there are less drunks among our people than any other".

To relate the idea of the Ember Days with the priestly ordinations, on the basement of the obelisks Gaudí placed the figure of three praying priests. On the North, or Advent, obelisk are the minor orders. On that of Lent or the East are subdeacons. On that of Whitsun or South are deacons, and that of September or West are priests.

As well as the four cardinal obelisks, there will be four central obelisks. Each one of them will bear three of the twelve verses of the hymn of Daniel about the young men in the fiery furnace of Babylon, which is recited in the ritual of the priestly ordination.

Drawing by Francesc Berenguer of the obelisk of the fire element of the Glory Façade.

Sacristies

The etymology of the word sacristy comes from "sacred", since it is the place where the sacred objects are kept. The Sagrada Família has two sacristies situated in the north and west corners of the cloister. The lanterns coincide with the cardinal points and link the virtues with the Ember Days, the four fasting periods that Christians practice corresponding to the four seasons, in gratitude for the fruits of the following season.

The lantern of winter, in the north, with the snake and the chest, symbolise prudence. That of autumn, in the west, with a helmet and cuirass, symbolise strength. That of summer, in the south, with scales and a sword, symbolise justice, and that of spring, in the east, shows temperance, through the knife, bread and *porrón* spouted drinking vessel, icons of rural Catalonia, from where Antoni Gaudí came from.

The dome of the sacristy shows us, like the other domes of the Sagrada Família, the Church's praise for and dedication to Jesus Christ. On the pinnacle of the top we find the figure of the vintager who treads alone, described by Isaiah in the *Hymns of the Ordinations*, and a lamb about to be sacrificed. Completing the decoration of the dome are the palms, the *Amen* and the invocations of the Apocalypse, *Benedictio, Claritas, Sapientia, Gratiarum actio, Honor, Virtus and Fortitudo*, spread out in a circle of scales.

Model of the Sacristy displayed in the Museum.

The exterior walls

Each of the side walls of the temple will finalise with a pediment of rampants, the side of which will be crowned with an elegant basket of fruit from Camp de Tarragona, from the architect's childhood: apples. Figs, almonds, cherries, pomegranates, etc. These fruits and leaves will abound all over the elements of the large window, in order to symbolise the source of fruits that the Holy Spirit sends to men.

Over each window the image of a founding saint will be placed: Ignatius Loyola, Joseph Calasanctius, Dominic of Osma, Peter Nolasc, Raymond of Pennafort, Francis of Paola, Theresa of Jesus, Joaquima Vedruna de Mas, Anthony Mary Claret, John Bosco, in order to symbolise the fertile vine shoot which receives the sap from the stock, following the representation and meaning of those that are placed in the apse.

Saint Ignatius Loyola.
Work of Manuel Cussachs.

The coats of arms of the trades involved in the construction of the Expiatory Temple of the Sagrada Família.

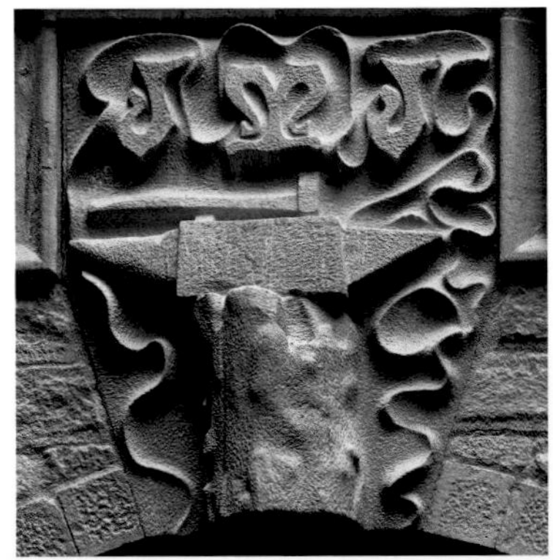

Large windows of the exterior walls of the Temple. With sculptures of Francesc Carulla and Joan Puigdollers.

PHILIPPU
APOSTOLUS
Sursum Corda
LA ENTRADA

Oració
GRUPS ESCOLARS
GRUPOS ESCOLARES
SCHOOL GROUPS

Pinnacles of the naves of the Temple crowned by fruits from the Tarragona countryside. Work of Etsuro Sotoo.

The bell towers and the domes

The bell towers are the most characteristic elements of the Sagrada Família. They are paraboloids of revolution, the most natural static form for a bell tower.

The symbolism of the bell tower, and in this case the bell towers of the Sagrada Família, participates in the general symbolism of the temple: a square or cube that turns into a spherical dome through the octagon or hexagon. To put it another way: the squaring of the circle. The towers start off with a square ground plan and one quarter way up the full height become round. The towers take part in the symbolism of the tortoise, which they take as a model, since the four legs of the tortoise are the square and the shell is the circular ground plan. The square is matter or earthly form, and is ruled by the number 4. The circle with a centre represents divinity or heaven, and is ruled by the number 1 —unity.

Just at the point of transition from the square to the circle, Gaudí places the image and name of the apostle to which each of the 12 bell towers is dedicated.

This sculptural series of each apostle is crowned by a constellation. The grand operation undertaken by the fathers of the Catholic Church of Christianising the pre-Christian or pagan myths, legends, festivals, etc. also reached the astrological constellations. As Bede the Venerable, the 8th-century English monk and encyclopaedist observed, the almost natural correspondence of the 12 constellations which obviously refer to the 12 months, would be the apostles, because 12 is the number of the wheel of life.

If we divide the 360° of a circumference into 12, we get 12 portions of 30° degrees. This division is also based on the number 7 (4 + 3), the number par excellence of the cycles (a week or a cycle of the moon —7 × 4—), since the circumference is divided into 4, the number of matter (4 cardinal points, 4 basic elements, etc.), and each one of the these fourths of 90° by 3, the spiritual number, and we have the 12 portions of 30°. If we reverse the process, the sum of these 12 portions gives us the circumference, an this is why all representations of the world that aim to be global or total use the circumference or wheel of life.

Even in the 8th century, Bede the Venerable wanted an apostle to correspond to each constellation, so that Aries would be Saint Peter, Taurus, Saint Andrew, and successively until completing the 12 signs of the Zodiac with the 12 apostles. Other constellations also had to Christianise their names: Andromeda would be Sepulchre, the Great Dog, David, and Hercules, the Magi of the Orient. These name changes proposed by Bede were not the result of a random choice. The English monk tried to find the symbolic equivalent, in the constellation, star or planet, in which we could call Christian mythology. Clearly his attempt was unsuccessful. In this case, the Christianisation of natural or pre-Christian religion did not work.

(Right page) Drawing by Francesc Berenguer.

Figure of the apostle Matthew on the Nativity Façade in the transition of the square ground plan to circular form.

JESUCRIST
173,00
ESTEL·LA MATUTINA
140,00
130,00
SANT LLUC
SANT JOAN

However, in the Sagrada Família Gaudí recovered this old project and placed the constellations of the Zodiac corresponding to each apostle on the Nativity Façade.

Progressing onto the symbology of the bell tower one can state that it is also a temple, though more stylised and outlined. It emphasises the upward aspect of the symbolism of the temple. The tower of a bell tower generally crowned by a spire is like a bridgehead between the earth and heaven. In this sense it is related to the symbolism of the cosmic mountain and is linked with the pyramids, the Sumerian ziggurats or the mountain-temples of Hinduism, clearly linked to the symbolism of the mountain. The fact that the building causes the maximum sense of verticality was an effect that they looked for and achieved in the Gothic cathedrals. The vertical impulse of the Gothic structures, of the pillars, arches and vaulting, transmit to the human being the sense of verticality and make them feel a key player between heaven and earth. A curved back is always associated with negative condition and bad luck, when the upright man looks up, he overcomes his human condition, tied to earth, and he comes closer to heaven. This idea is strengthened with the reading of the *Sanctus* written on the outside of the tower, which unfailingly obliges the man to raise their eyes towards heaven.

Menhir at Champ Dolent
Menhir at Champ Dolent in Dol-de-Bretagne.

The *Sanctus, Sanctus, Sanctus...*, ordered spirally, are dedicated, three at a time, to the Father, the Son and the Holy Spirit. The first, dedicated to the Father, will be yellow, the colour that best represents light; the second dedicated to the Holy Spirit, will be orange, and the third, dedicated to the Son, will be red, the colour used in the liturgy as a symbol of martyrdom. The Holy Spirit is in the centre because it is the communication between the Father and the Son, and its colour is the result of the other two. These inscriptions will constitute a type of spiral ribbon that will climb up the towers. Everyone that reads them, even non-believers, will intone a hymn to the Holy Trinity as they gradually discover its content: the *Sanctus, Sanctus, Sanctus...* will draw their eyes towards heaven.

Plaster model of a pinnacle.

We see three comments by Gaudí about the bell towers:

(*a*) "The form of the towers, vertical and parabolic, is the union between gravity and light. At the highest point will be the well-lit spotlights; like natural light, which also comes from the sky. The spotlights, of which we have already spoken, will provide life and magnificence to the temple on nights of religious services and at the same time form the best ornament in the city".

(*b*) "Now, at the top, there are still some letters missing. They will be of different sizes, so that the observer gradually discovers them as they get closer. These sizes will be the result of a calculation. The sight appreciates things up to a distance of 500 diameters if the object is opaque and, if it is shiny, up to 1,000 diameters. In the inscriptions the letters will be between 40 cm and 1 metre high.

The smallest will be able to be seen from nearby the temple and the others from further away. Observations made say that the highest cross will be seen comfortably from 2,000 metres away. The diameter is three metres and the surface is shiny".

(*c*) "Look at this end!... Doesn't it seem to join earth with heaven? This explosion of mosaics will be the first that navigators approaching Barcelona will see: it will be a radiant welcome! I am satisfied with the final model of the naves, but I would be annoyed if i could not produce a complete section and would lament like.

Pinnacles that crown the Nativity Façade.

Angel carrying a mitre from the Episcopal Palace of Astorga
In 1889, Gaudí designed three angels that should have crowned the palace, each one carrying a bishop's attribute.

Da Vinci: What beautiful things there would be if only there were the means!".

The highest tower, that representing Jesus Christ, will measure 170 metres, approximately the same height as the mountain of Montjuïc. Gaudí's original idea was for it to be the tallest building in the city.

The 18 towers, which represent the 12 apostles of Jesus Christ (100 metres), the four evangelists, the Virgin Mary —the tower of the apse— and Jesus Christ —the tower of the transept—, are also menhirs that place the world here below in contact with the world beyond above. When on the 30 November 1925, the construction of the first tower of the Nativity Façade was completed, the first on the left, dedicated to Saint Barnabus, Gaudí expressed his joy commenting that it was "like a spear that joined heaven and earth".

The menhirs, however, also regulate the telluric energy. Just like the needles in acupuncture regulate the energy channels of the human body, the construction of menhirs, which human beings have made since distant times, is also a type of acupuncture for the planet Earth.

The bell towers of the Sagrada Família would be the peaks of the mountain that is the temple. The formal similarity, already noted by Verdaguer, with the mountain of Montserrat, is clear.

The pinnacles that culminate the towers are very colourful and symbolically present the characteristic elements of the bishops: ring, crozier, mitre and cross. With this symbolism Gaudí reproduces with expressiveness the liturgy, since the bishops are the successors to the apostles, and therefore it is logical that the attributes of the bishops culminate the towers of the apostles.

The main bell tower, which will culminate the dome, will be the tower representing Jesus Christ, crowned by a six-armed cross and a lamb.

Gaudí liked these crosses very much, and they are present in other buildings by the architect. They strengthen the quaternary symbolism that all crosses posses, because the four horizontal arms show the four cardinal points. It is like a cross in volume, in three dimensions. It is the ideal cross for the architect-geometrist that Gaudí was. The sunrays will make the mosaics of this large cross shine every day, and artificial light will be projected onto the other bell towers during the night.

Very close to this main tower is the one that represents the Virgin, crowned by a luminous star, *Stella Matutina*.

A little more separated we come across the four towers representing the four evangelists, crowned by the animals that symbolise them: an angel, a bull, a lion and an eagle. Look carefully at the correspondence with the axiom, the basis of all initiation study, and already pointed out by Zoroaster of knowing, wanting, daring and remaining silent:

(*a*) Knowing the truth of the mystery, the truth of life, the truth of the spirit, visible thanks to universal gravitation.

(*b*) Wanting justice, through sacrifice, to achieve harmony and progress of freedom.

On the pinnacles, Gaudí brought together and synthesised the three symbolic attributes of bishops: mitre, staff and ring.

(*c*) Daring by following absolute faith, in the balance of the body that can be modified by deliberation.

(*d*) Remaining silent about the reality of the dogma, action of the perfectible soul by antagonism.

Knowledge corresponds to the angel, intelligence. Wanting is symbolised by the body of the bull, it is work. Daring is the lion, which embodies spirit. And remaining silent is symbolised by the wings of the eagle. To obtain wisdom or knowledge, one must want and it is necessary to dare; once this knowledge has been attained, the only thing remaining is to remain silent.

These four personifications (angel, bull, lion and eagle) correspond to the four evangelists as well as the four signs of the Zodiac that form a Greek cross —the four equal arms— within a circumference and to the four basic elements: air, earth, fire and water. The correspondences are the following:

(*a*) Knowing/Aquarius; sign of air/angel or human figure (the figure of the water carrier); it relates to Jesus Christ or God made into man. It is Saint Matthew.

(*b*) Wanting/Taurus; sign of land/bull or ox; the bull is the animal of sacrifices and the Gospel of Luke deals extensively with the sacrifice of Jesus Christ on the cross. It is Saint Luke.

(*c*) Daring/Leo; sign of fire/lion; because this evangelist began with the preaching of the Baptist, the voice that cries out in the desert. It is Saint Mark.

(*d*) Remain silent/Scorpion; sign of water/eagle (in this sign the elliptical crosses the scorpion and the eagle: "From the blind scorpion that challenges the eagle to fly around the high spheres"); the eagle refers to the high spiritual content of this evangelist, since according to the bestiary it is the only animal that can look at the sun (symbolically God) face on. It is Saint John.

The four domes of the four evangelists will project two beams of light at night, one towards the earth, to symbolise the Gospel that enlightens man, and the other toward the central dome, to represent the divinity and superiority of Jesus Christ.

Constellations that crown the sculptures of the apostles.

(Right page) Sculptural series (in this case dedicated to the apostle Simon) that shows the transition of the ground plan of the bell towers.

The spiral staircases

The ascension to the mountain-temples of Egypt, India, China or pre-Columbian America was like making a journey to the symbolic "centre of the world". In this sense, the symbolism of the stairway is also related to the symbolism of the tree.

The climb up the stairway enables a change of level, of register, passing from a profane space to a sacred one. Thus, the natural location of temples is the peak of the mountains, the highest point. Hermitages are often found at the top of mountains or in high spots.

One of the symbols of the stairway is that of spiritual evolution by stages or states. It is the *scala dei*. The spiral stairways of the towers of the Sagrada Família are heirs to this architectural tradition of temple-mountain that has its origin in Sumer. The bell towers of the Sagrada Família are like ziggurats that enable one to transcend the profane space, the earthly space. The spiral stairway is, in fact, the most perfect and spiritual way of climbing there is, since we rise up through a circular movement. The movement we make on a spiral stairway also reminds us of the dances of the swirling dervishes.

(Right page)
Drawing of the interior of a bell tower and model of one of the tubular bells that Gaudí thought of placing inside the towers.

Overhead view of the spiral staircase of one of the towers of the Nativity Façade.

The bells

The sound of a bell always symbolises the power of the creator, and who wields this power in the first and last instant is God. A splendid and beautiful text says, "When the bells peal, it is God speaking". The bells are also the instruments that make it possible for Jesus Christ to be the chronocrator, the lord of time.

The fact that the bells are placed at the highest point of churches, the bell tower —apart from the practical function of sounding out—, also strengthen, due to their height, the symbol of belonging to divinity: they are the voice of God. The very shape of the bells, similar to that of the heavenly vaulting, reinforces this relationship with divinity.

The bells of churches or temples are often hanging, so they also take part in the mystical symbolism of objects that hang between heaven and earth.

As is well known, sounds are essential and basic elements of the rite in all traditions and religions. They are also important elements for all the peoples, from Chinese gongs to today's electrical bells. In these cases the sounds mark and point out the cyclical rhythm, that is, time. We could say, however, that the sound of the bells is in some way an opposite and complementary sound to that of the drums, which are also rhythm of the cycles and fundamental elements of rites. So if the drum represents the beats of the earth or of telluric energy, then the sound of the bell is the beat of heaven or of cosmic energy. One is the sound of matter; the other, of the spirit.

The sound of the bells in the Sagrada Família was one of Gaudí's great concerns, something that led him to make an in-depth study of everything related to bells and acoustic physics.

The fact that the towers, the most emblematic and characteristic element of the Sagrada Família, are bell towers, gives us an idea of the importance he afforded them. In total there will be 84 bells. On the Nativity Façade he placed tubular percussion bells; on that of the Passion, tubular organ bells, which will sound with injected air, and on the Glory Façade, bells tuned to the notes of E, G and C, the easiest notes to obtain. Moreover, the bells of the Nativity and Passion façades, which will contain the notes, will be able to played like a piano or harmonium.

The stone blinds characteristic of the upper part of the bell towers are designed to favour the diffusion of sound given off by the bells. When all the bells of the Sagrada Família sound, we will be able to say without doubt that we are listening to celestial music.

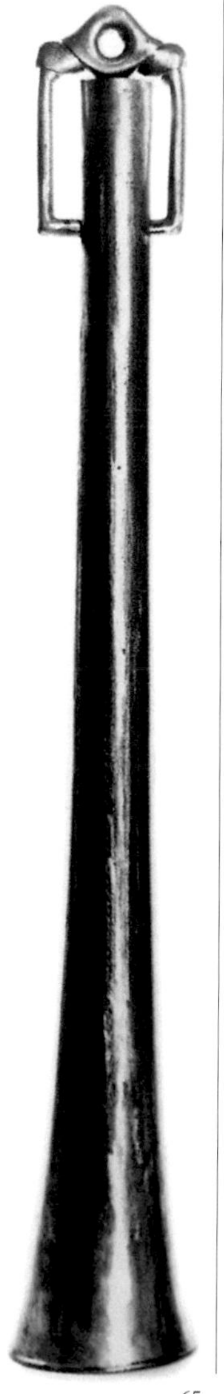

Relief of the central altar of the crypt that represents the Holy Family, by Josep Llimona.

The crypt

All crypts share the symbolism of the cave, the cavern. This rich symbolism refers to both the maternal womb, the beginning of life or centre of the world —the case of the crypt—, and the representation of the underworld or sub-world.

The work crypt comes from the Greek *kriptós*, which means "hidden", "occult". It is the cave, mother earth; it is cosmic fertility or original source of life. In ancient times, subterranean chambers of the temples housed images of the god Isis. With the introduction of Christianity, these images became Black Virgins. It is therefore absolutely logical that on the dome of the crypt of the Sagrada Família the Annunciation of Mary is represented and that the chapel of the Assumption of Mary occupies a privileged place in the crypt.

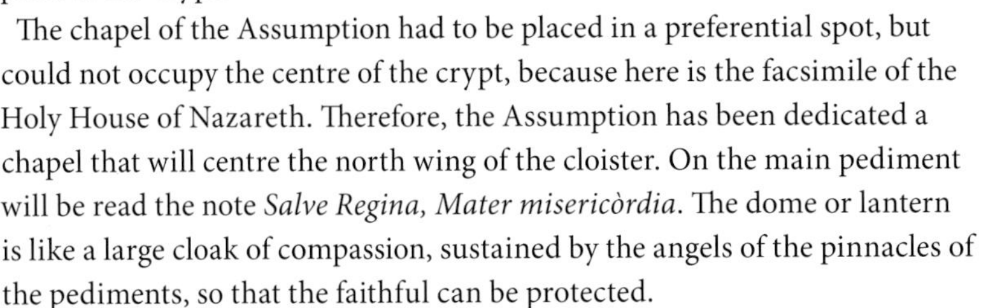

The chapel of the Assumption had to be placed in a preferential spot, but could not occupy the centre of the crypt, because here is the facsimile of the Holy House of Nazareth. Therefore, the Assumption has been dedicated a chapel that will centre the north wing of the cloister. On the main pediment will be read the note *Salve Regina, Mater misericòrdia*. The dome or lantern is like a large cloak of compassion, sustained by the angels of the pinnacles of the pediments, so that the faithful can be protected.

In the interior, the Trinity crowns Mary and rises to heaven surrounded by the angelic hierarchies: seraphs, cherubs and the archangels Saint Michael and Saint Gabriel. The angels form a crown in the gallery and twelve of them —the number of the totality of the circle, the number of the circle—, the stars of the crown of the Virgin, carry fruits instead of flowers: they are the fruits of the Holy Spirit.

Beneath the gallery there will be four representations of the life of Mary: her death, her life with Saint Joseph, the presentation of Mary in the temple by Joachim and Anne, her parents, and the miracle of the wedding of Canaan, performed by Jesus Christ at the behest of his mother.

The seven chapels of the crypt are dedicated to the members of the Holy Family of Jesus Christ: Sacred Heart, Immaculate Conception, Saint Joseph, Saint Joaquin and Saint Anne, Saint Elizabeth and Saint Zachariah, Saint John the Baptist and Saint John the Evangelist. The mosaic shows the vine and wheat, clearly coherent with the symbolism of deep fertility, since the two fruits are Mediterranean symbols of fertility. The high altar shows us the liturgical time of Easter, with a relief by Josep Llimona dedicated to the Holy Family.

(Right page, below) Medallion of the keystone of the central vaulting of the crypt by the sculptor Joan Flotats. It shows the Annunciation to Mary.

Detail of mosaic on the ground that represents a bird eating a grape seed, by the mosaic artist Mario Maragliano.

Nativity Façade

"We have made a complete façade of the temple, so that its importance makes it impossible to not continue the work".

Antoni Gaudí

Some people argue it is inspired by a peculiar underwater baroque style. This is what Rubió i Tudurí believed when he designed the gardens of Plaça Gaudí with the lake that provides the reflection of the façade, thus emphasising the "soft" and multiform aspects of the volumes. The secret of this façade, however, is in the paradoxical effect of movement that the stone transmits. It is as if the sculptures move.

It is made up of three doorways dedicated to the theological virtues of Faith, Hope and Charity, the central and tallest one being the Charity doorway. Moreover, these three doorways are dedicated to, respectively, Saint Joseph, the Virgin Mary and the Baby Jesus, and parallel to the early years of Jesus Christ: background or origins, childhood and adolescence. The four bell towers represent, from right to left, Saint Matthias, Saint Judas, Saint Simon and Saint Barnabus.

According to Gaudí's project, this façade had to be polychrome. As regards the figures, on the lower level (the pedestals) is represented the anecdote of the Christmas cockerels and turkeys, followed by the most popular events from Jesus' childhood in Christian iconography: the Flight to Egypt, the Slaughter of the Innocents, the Nativity, the Visitation and the meeting of the Baby Jesus in the temple. Higher up, the three important events in chronological order: the Wedding, the Annunciation and the Presentation. Then, the symbolic pinnacles of the theological virtues and, to end, at the top of the bell towers, the invocation of the group of angels: *Sanctus*... and *Hosanna in excelsis*...

1 Nativity façade

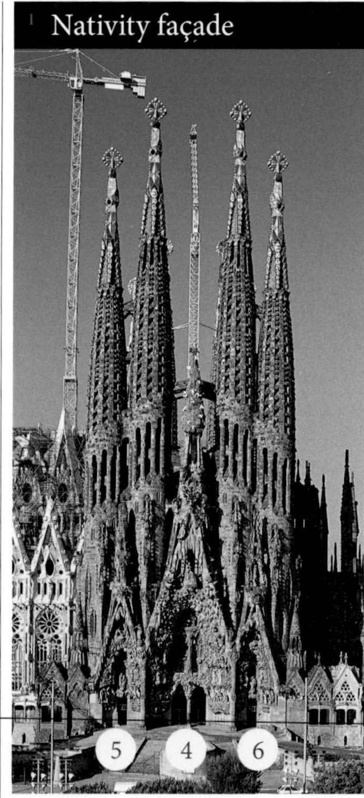

4 Charity Doorway
5 Hope Doorway
6 Faith Doorway

Sanctus
Sanctus
Sanctus

4

Charity Doorway

It is the central doorway, also called that of Christian Love. All the figures comment on the virtue of charity. Around the nativity scene, the totality of the cosmos praises the son of God. On the lintel of the doors, written in majestic letters, one reads: *Gloria in excelsis Deo et in terra pax hominibus bonae voluntatis.*

All the paintings and images refer to the birth and infancy of the Baby Jesus. The ox and the mule provide the child with warmth; the shepherds and the three Kings of the Orient adore him, and the angels transmit the new good. The central column, which divides the door into two, has the snake with the apple in the mouth wound up at the base, symbolising original sin. The response to the "fall" of mankind was the coming to the world of the Baby Jesus to save humanity. Made up of a sheaf of palms joined by a spiral strip, the column bears the genealogy of Jesus and on the upper part the whole Nativity scene is depicted.

The very arrangement of the column or pillar is an evocative description of the above: thanks for the coming to the world of the Baby Jesus —capital or upper part of the column— mankind can overcome and transcend the state in which he had fallen —column or pillar in itself— after the original sin or "fall" —base of the pillar. In many religions and traditions the human being starts from an idyllic and harmonious situation, such as that of Adam and Eve in paradise, later falling into a situation of imperfection due to a serious mistake or original sin.

Over the archivolt, the annunciation of the archangel to Mary represents the act of sublime love through which the Virgin Mary collaborates with the divine work. Higher up, the coronation of Mary as queen and empress is the prize with which the Trinity corresponds to the virginal offering. The group of angels behind the Virgin por out between flowers the *Sanctus, Sanctus, Sanctus Deus.* Like all the angels that Gaudí placed on this façade, they do not have wings.

Above the cave of the Coronation is placed the anagram of the name of Jesus over a cross in a cloud. Nevertheless, the symbolic summary of this doorway is the pinnacle: a pelican, primitive Eucharistic symbol, feeding its young at the foot of an eternally green and incorruptible cypress tree, shelter of birds (doves) during the storm, which culminates in the Tau, the Greek initial of the name of God. Two ladders lean against the cypress, at the feet of which there are two angels with an amphora and a breadbasket.

The flora on this doorway features eighteen species: acacia, Judas tree, hydrangea, palms, wisteria, lilies, Japanese golden lily, water lily, reed lily, fleur-de-lis, alfalfa, Jesse tree, olive, almond, apricot, peach, cherry and apple trees.

25
27
24
Sanctus
26
22
23
21
20
30
19
17
18
10
10
16
15
15
7
7
8
8
12
14
13
11
9
9

The two columns

Although it is not the main entrance to the temple, the columns of the Charity Doorway take part in the rich symbolism of the two columns that support the entrance to all temples. Facing the façade, the column on the left is dedicated to Joseph and the one on the right to Mary. The most famous columns of the temple are those that overlooked the entrance to the temple of Jerusalem or the temple of King Solomon, known as Solomonic columns. According to the Masonic tradition, the column on the left is that of the Brothers, and has engraved the secret word of this level, J.·., and the column on the right is that which corresponds to the level of apprentice and bears the secret word of this level, B.·..

All columns symbolise the nexus between this here below and that which is there above. In this sense, the symbolism is similar to that of the stairway or tree. Situated at the temple door, the Solomonic columns constitute the nexus between the profane world —that which is outside the temple— and the sacred world —that which is inside the temple. In reality, they are the threshold or frontier between these two worlds.

They also take part in the symbolism of the cosmic duality or bipolarity, linked to the number 2. The overcoming of this cosmic duality is achieved in the sacred space that is the temple. Only by entering inside it can one move from 2 to 3.

Detail of the names inscribed on the columns of the Charity Doorway.

Ornamental spirals halfway up the column.

(Right page) Columns of the Charity Doorway dedicated to Joseph and Mary as pillars on which is placed the Gospel.

8

Chameleons

The main symbolic function of the chameleon is that of intermediary between God and the human being, or between heaven and earth. In many myths and legends about the creation of the world, this animal plays a relevant role, because in these cosmologies it climbs to the crowns of the tallest trees and, as a consequence, is the being that is closest to God.

The chameleon, however, stands out above all for its adaptation to the environment through its great ability to transform its external aspect or appearance. Therefore, as well as representing the eternal process of development or movement of nature, it is also the symbol of the best antidote to paralysis: only by changing and transforming the accessory, apparent and circumstantial, can we maintain the substantial and immutable, in other words, the eternal.

According to other legends, the chameleon has seven other properties that are also seven symbols: (1) it changes colour, so it has great power of transformation, enabling it to adapt to any situation; (2) its tongue, long and retractile, enabling it to act at a distance and withdraw in time; (3) it moves slowly and never face on, it is a wonder of prudence and precaution; (4) when it gathers information about the place it finds itself in, it never turns its back, but swivels its head, moves its eyes and analyses everything that surrounds it; (5) it has a body compressed sideways which makes it extremely agile; (6) The dorsal crest is used for defence, and (7) the prehensile tail enables it to hunt the animals that it feeds off. These seven qualities are of great use for any being.

Chameleon of the Hope Doorway.

9

Tortoises

On the Nativity Façade the tortoises are the Atlases that support the two columns of the Charity Doorway. According to zoologists, the tortoise on the side of the sea is marine and the one of the side of the mountain a land tortoise. In what is substantial, this situation does not affect the symbolism of the tortoise.

The function of Atlas of the tortoise fits perfectly with its main symbolism: primordial strength over which the cosmos rests. In this sense, it is fully coherent that in the base of the columns that support the birth of Jesus Christ there are tortoises. For a believer like Gaudí, what could have been more basic and primordial than the birth of God made into man?

The tortoise is the conjunction between the square and the circle. In this primordial tortoise, the square and earthly material supports the round and celestial shell. The four legs of the tortoise would be the four pillars that represent the four cardinal points, and the shell, the vaulting of heaven. This is a solid symbol of the cosmos in its non-transcendent aspect. In diverse mythologies, the tortoise supports the earth; therefore, it is both the image of the cosmos and the stabilising element of this selfsame cosmos. In the last analysis, the tortoise symbolises a corporeal nature, very true of the façade in which God becomes man.

Turtle (below) and tortoise (right).

(Right page, above) Chameleon of Faith Doorway stalking a fly.

8

9

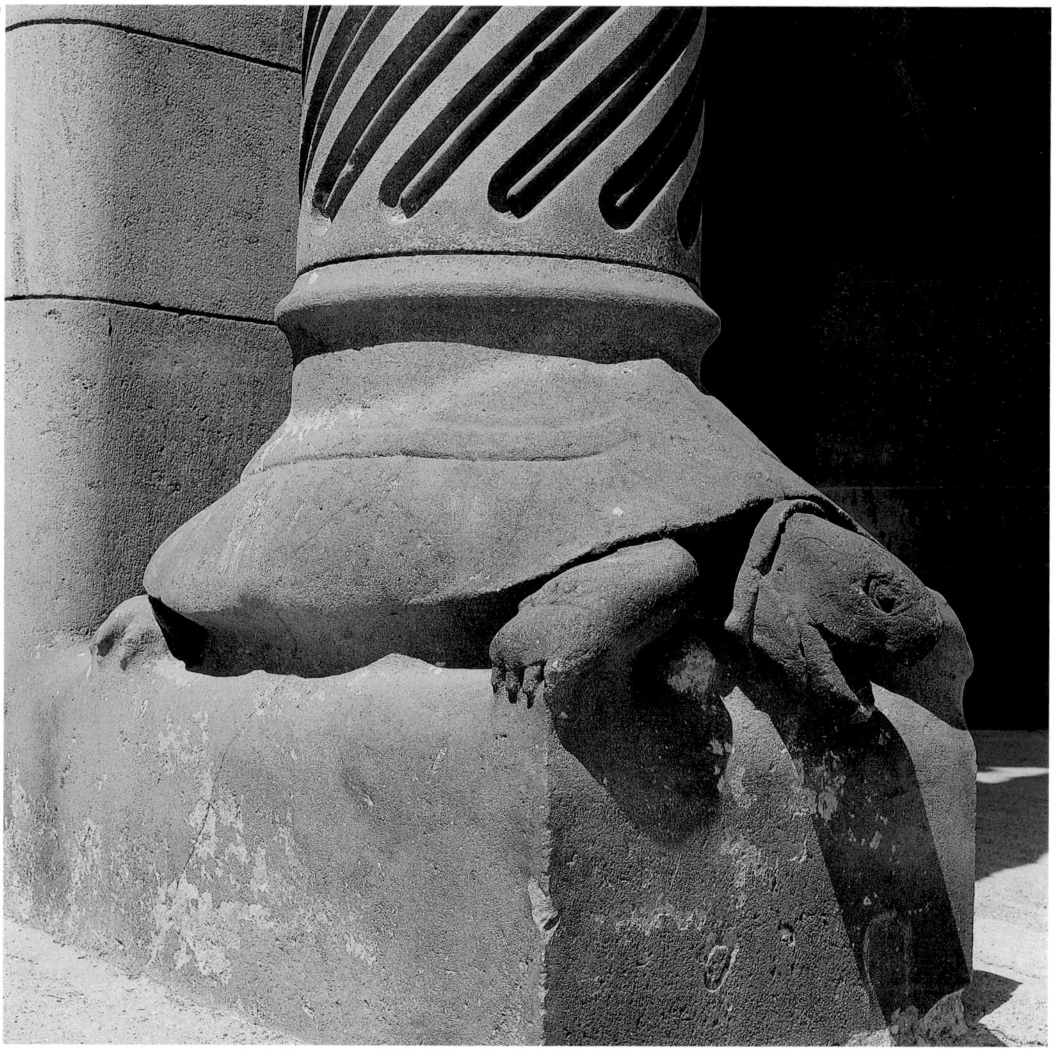

Angels of the Final Judgement

Both angels from the Final Judgement crown the columns of the Charity Doorway dedicated to Joseph and Mary. The distinctive attribute of the angels of the Final Judgement are the trumpets, since their sound, as well as calling out or warning humanity of the holding of the judgement, also represent the rebirth of true life, after the trial, since death is equivalent to the death of the soul or of the transcendent finality of humankind. The tomb is the body and desires, or corporal hunger. The angel "awakens", with their light and the sound of the trumpet, the sleeping desire for resurrection of the fallen man. From the golden trumpets comes the voice of God, who calls out the victory of the spirit over matter.

These angels are positioned over some strange and large balls. The solar symbolism of the angels of the Apocalypse, represented by the gilded trumpets, is complemented by their golden hair. The golden curls that can find in many iconographic representations of angels or in descriptions in some texts, do not obey any rule of Anglo-Saxon or top-model beauty, they simply emphasise their solar symbolism.

Cathedral of Strasbourg
Drawings of the construction plan where we see the announcing angels represented. It seems that Gaudí made a journey in his youth around France to study its cathedrals.

Pair of angels that culminate the column dedicated to Mary (left). Detail of the announcing angel of the Final Judgement, for which the illustrator Opisso was model (above).

Pair of angels on the apex of the column dedicated to Joseph (right). Work of Llorenç Matamala.

Central column

On this central column of the Charity Doorway, and therefore of the Nativity Façade, once again the Gaudian idea is fulfilled of the Temple of the Sagrada Família as a meeting space between the descendent forces or realities, from heaven to earth, and the ascending forces, from earth to heaven —cosmic energy and telluric energy, respectively.

The snake climbing the column with the apple in the mouth represents original sin and the fall of mankind, something that is found in the origin of the birth of the son of God (we are in the Nativity Façade), given that if the original sin had not existed, God would not have had to become man, because the aim of Jesus Christ is to bring the message of salvation.

On the same column, going downwards, we find the name of Jesus' forebears, as from the grand patrician Abraham. This Christian genealogy, as well as showing us that the remedy or response to the fall of mankind is the message of faith in Christ, it shows us —and this aspect is fundamental in my opinion— that the action of sending the son to save us is not an isolated and unique event but something that obeys a planned action that is framed within a divine plan that obviously surpasses the strict frontiers of the Catholic religion.

The snake is one of the animals with the richest symbolic content. To start with it represents a total opposition to the human being, both genetically and symbolically. If man were placed at the end of a long genetic chain of animal evolution, at the other end would be the snake. The snake is basic and instinctive energy. Energy in pure state.

If human aspiration is to raise oneself and free oneself of earthly ties, the snake is a carrier of the lowest and most earthly; we should not forget that it is a reptile and therefore abject. It has often been stated that the symbolism of the snake is ambivalent, and we have already said that from the symbolic point of view it is polysemic and that Christianity has remained with only the most negative symbolism. This then, is the reading that should be made of the snake of earthly Paradise that appears entwined around the column of the Nativity Façade and that tricked Adam and Eve. The one associated with evil, with Satan, with the devil, the one condemned to crawl for eternity and which represents all the vices, which brings us closer to death and distances us from eternal life. The apple strengthens this symbolism, since it represents earthly desires, among them that of the knowledge of our forefathers.

The prophets and divine messengers that obviously drop from heaven are the antidote for the snake's venom. This is the central column that supports the birth of Jesus Christ.

Detail of the name "Jesus" inscribed on the central column.

(Right page) Central column and detail of the names of the genealogy of Jesus central.

Snake with the apple in the mouth that represents original sin.

12

The ox and the mule

From the symbolic perspective, the ox and the mule of the Nativity represent the basic and essential polarity. Remember, however, that originally the scriptures talk of the ox and the ass. Although from a symbolic point of view the mule and the ass are practically the same, and only the desire to remove from the sublime act of the birth of the Messiah any negative connotation that could be associated with the ass, it was converted into a mule, so for symbolic purposes this transformation is totally irrelevant.

In the case of the birth in the manger, the ox and the mule represent the cosmic duality present in the manifest world. We should not forget that in our culture, the birth of God is —obviously— the most sublime moment of divine manifestation. The ox symbolises the charitable efforts and the mule the evil efforts, they are good and evil. In this sense they take part in the almost infinite dualities of the manifest world: black-white, masculine-feminine, above-below, cold-hot, yin-yang, etc.

This same symbolism is present at the moment of death of Jesus Christ, on either side of the cross, with the good thief and the bad thief.
Once again the cosmic duality of good and evil.

The itinerary of God made into man begins and ends with the same symbolic concept, characteristic of the manifest or material world, at the moment of the birth, represented by two animals, which, as such, symbolise good and evil in brute force or strength, true of all birth. At the moment of death, in contrast, who embodies these two concepts are two human beings, who have experienced the possibility of good and evil. The ox and the mule are good and evil in the making, like any mortal at the moment of being born, inasmuch as the two thieves are good and evil already realised. The life cycle shows this and it could not be any other way.

Details of the ox and mule from the sculptural group of the birth of baby Jesus.

The sculptural group of the Nativity becomes the central point towards which the looks of all the figures of this doorway are directed. Work of Jaume Busquets.

13

The shepherds of the Adoration

For nomadic and cattle-rearing peoples, the figure of shepherd is heavy with religious symbolism. God is the main shepherd, since the flock symbolises the cosmic forces. Nevertheless, God delegates his functions to other shepherds who exercise both temporal and religious power; they are the shepherds of the people. More than kings, governors, judges, priests, etc., we must talk of shepherds, pastors, since all these posts must be shepherds that watch over their flock.

The shepherd is the symbol of intuitive and experimental knowledge that appears only in pure men. It also symbolises the state of vigil, the maximum attention for everything that is occurring. For this reason, they are the first to come and adore, to recognise the birth of the son of God, because they are alert to events, to the angel that wakes them and informs them the Messiah has been born. Some pseudo-social interpretations have pointed to the shepherds as the first who came to adore the baby Jesus because of the will of the son of God is to be amongst the poorest and humblest. Symbolically, this makes no sense. Like when the angel wakes the shepherds to go and adore the Baby Jesus, they have remained asleep because they were very tired, it is simply that the angel reveals to them the new reality that represents the arrival of the Messiah on earth. Equally, when the apostles and disciples stay sleeping in the garden of Gethsemane, shortly before Jesus Christ is arrested, it is not that they are tired and drop to the ground exhausted, it is simply that they are not aware of the importance of the events they are experiencing; they remain asleep to that reality.

The shepherd is also the wise and errant pilgrim of other traditions, such as the errant dervishes, who wander around the world rootless and survive thanks to charity. It is the enlightened wise man of so many tales that is hidden behind the humble figure of the beggar that we find in the town square.

Figures related to the rich Catalan nativity scene tradition.

Three kings of the Orient

The three kings of the Orient, the three wise men, present in the adoration of the Baby Jesus, were three priests of the Zoroaster religion, Zoroastrism, also known as Mazdaism. This priestly class possessed deep knowledge of magic and astrology. For the Greeks, *mago* was the priest of the Zoroaster religion. When Saint Matthew wrote the word *magos*, he did not do it using the current meaning of the word, but referred to those wise oriental or Mede priests.

The extensive knowledge of astrology —remember, among other things, the ziggurats were temples and astrological observatories, or it was them who left us the 12 signs of the Zodiac as we know them today— enabled them to understand and interpret the meaning of the star. The astrological reality of the star was a Jupiter-Saturn conjunction in the sign of Pisces, which indicated the exceptional nature of the person born under that sign. The birth of Jesus Christ inaugurated the era of Pisces, replaced recently by the sign of Aquarius.

The knowledge of how to interpret the dream they had had but did not inform Herod of, that they had found the Baby Jesus, since Herod's intention was probably infanticide.

The tradition according to which Melchior, Caspar and Balthazar were the white, blonde and black Kings respectively, indicates that it was the whole of humanity —all races— that adored the Messiah.

The symbolism of these three magi-priests and of their offerings is very rich. The sculptures of the façade represent the three kings at the time of the adoration. In an early symbolic interpretation, gold symbolises the power of the kings, frankincense the divine adoration and myrrh the very suffering of the human condition. With this offering, they recognised the coexistence, in that child, of royal power, divine majesty and human nature.

A deeper reading, however, leads us to the following interpretation. The gold that Melchior offers represents alchemy, the science of human transmutation. Symbolically it is associated with the sun, another central element and very rich symbolically. However, gold and the sun are also associated with fire, the transforming element par excellence.

The frankincense of King Caspar is astrology, the science that governs the life of men. The influence of the stars on men is realised through the air element and the frankincense is linked to this element.

The myrrh of King Balthazar is magic, the science of transformation or acting in the material world, associated with the element of water.

Thus, a symbolic reading of the three Magi shows us the profound possibility of transformation or growth that the birth of the Baby Jesus offered humankind. The triad of Melchior-alchemy, Caspar-astrology and Balthazar-magic enables the following interpretation: the union of the science "from here below" (magic) with the science "of there above" (astrology) leads to the transformation or transmutation of the human being (alchemy).

Another reading may also be made, according to which the gold is the earth, the myrrh the heart and the frankincense the spirit or spirituality.

Details of the offerings of the Magic Kings: Balthazar-myrrh.

Caspar-incense.

Melchior-gold.

Musician angels

Six angels play diverse instruments: harp, bassoon, violin, guitar, bagpipes and tambourine. They provide the celestial music to the painting of the nativity and the adoration, since they are the perfect messengers that travel between the celestial and earthly levels; and, furthermore, they are messengers that always bring good news.

It is well known that there are many types of angels, by hierarchy and by speciality. In this case they are musician angels, and of the six instruments they are playing, three are representative of worshiping music and three of popular music, as if Gaudí, mixing them fifty-fifty, wanted to give a sense of totality and that this ensemble of six musicians was in some way representative of all types of music, a perfect synthesis of musical vibration. Symbolically, the harp, violin and guitar are three practically synonymous string instruments, maintaining some difference or specialisation within a general symbolism. The harp is a traditional instrument par excellence and symbolically connects heaven and earth. The guitar is symbolically identified with the lyre, which is the instrument of cosmic harmony. The bassoon is identified with the horn, symbol of male power, but it is not only a symbol of temporal power, it is above all the spiritual power that is produced from the relationship with God; in this case the relationship between the Son and the Father is obvious. The tambourine is associated with the drum, which represents the deep rhythm of the universe, and even more so the small drum, which connotes light music and dance. The bagpipes or hunting horn is a wind instrument associated with origins, purity and innocence.

These six angels also have the function, on either side of the Baby Jesus, of celestial court. They are "the court of the king of the heavens", or also the army of the king of kings.

Musician angels who surround the Nativity scene, work of the Japanese sculptor Etsuro Sotoo.

16

The star

Stars are always an element that symbolically puts the two worlds in contact with each other, that of here below and that of beyond above; it is one of the infinite number of ways that divinity has of expressing itself in the earthly world in order to interrelate the two levels.

The star of the Nativity is the sign of heaven, of the world up above, for the inhabitants of the world here below, that announces the birth of the Messiah, the son of God. The three magicians and astrologists from the Orient are able to read and interpret this message correctly.

There are several theories about the astronomical reality of this star, but according to the latest hypothesis it was a supernova and a triple conjunction of Jupiter-Saturn, which took place in 7 BC in the constellation of Pisces. It had to be in this constellation because, as is known, Jesus Christ is the incarnation of the astrological period of Pisces. Whatever the case, it was a message from heaven to mortals.

The star of this façade is in a central and overhead position regarding the whole of the Nativity scene, and therefore indicates a clear correspondence between the celestial and earthly planes. In this position, emphasis is also made on the identification between star and angel, since the star is like a protective angel of the birth of the Baby Jesus (remember that the angels are the natural inhabitants of the intermediate world, the symbolic space between heaven and earth).

However, the composition of this sculptural series draws the father-mother-child-star axis, which underlines the identification between the child and the star. Making a more transcendent reading that identifies the Eucharist with the birth of Jesus Christ, we would say that Joseph is the priest, Mary the altar, Jesus Christ the Holy Form of Divine Host (the Body of Christ) and the star the vaulting of heaven or natural temple. The star is, therefore, the centre of the universe or spiritual axis of the world. We can say that the birth of Baby Jesus symbolically causes the creation of the first temple.

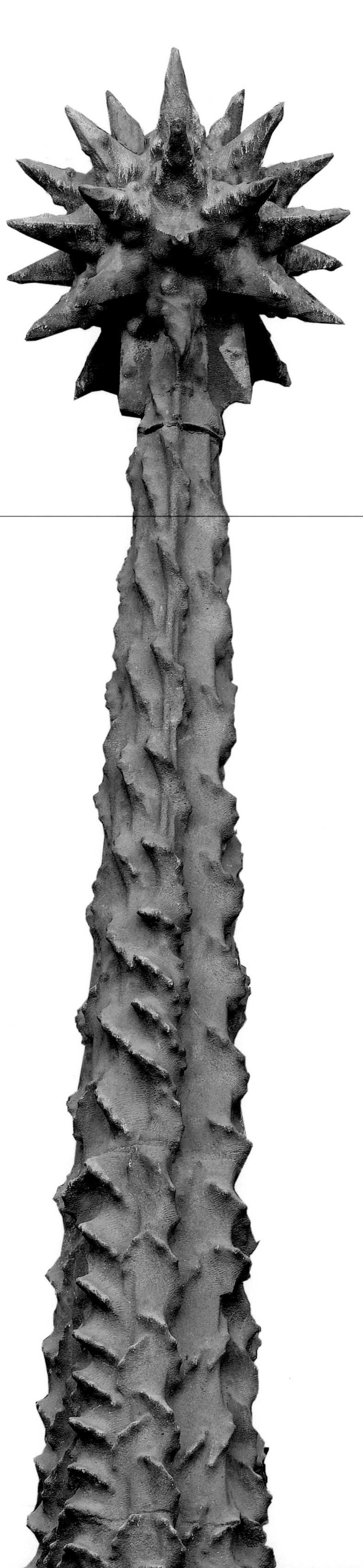

Detail of the star of the Charity Doorway that announces the birth of the Baby Jesus. Over the Nativity and around the star, a choir of child angels. Work of Etsuro Sotoo (right).

17

Rosary

Framing the sculptural group of the Incarnation there is a monumental rosary. Rosaries, with other names, are common in many traditions and religions. In general, all of them have the function of providing rhythm to prayer, always based on the vital basic rhythm: the respiration. Apart from being a help for the memory and acting as a mnemotechnical support, the rhythmical repetition of a sound or a word usually produces a state of rapture similar to musical experience.

In essence, a rosary is a thread with some parts or moving beads. In the Hindu rosary or *mala*, the beads are often pearls that symbolise all the states of the manifest world, and the thread symbolises the vital breath that crosses and joins the elements of this manifestation. It has 50 beads, which are the fifty letters of the Sanskrit alphabet. The Muslim rosary has 99 beads, representing the 99 names of God, which in reality is 100 because there is a name of secret God, which is no other than the representation of the return of multiplication (99) of the unit (1) or of the manifestation of the beginning. The Buddhist rosary from India has 108 beads (12 × 9), the cyclical number that represents the gestation or development of the manifest world, since 12 is the number of the global representation of the cosmos and 9 is the number of gestation. In the Christian tradition, the rosary, the origin of which is attributed to Saint Dominic de Guzmán, possesses 50 beads separated in groups of ten by another larger one, and its ends are joined by a cross, thus totalling 54 beads (half of the oriental rosary of 108 beads).

The Turkish *komboloi* or *tashbi* are even more present in the Islamic world. Although for many users it has lost the strictly religious function, contact with the most common material of the beads, amber or *elektron*, absorbs negative psychosomatic aspects, both for those pray and those who just run the beads through their fingers.

The rosary is identified with the wheel due to its closed circular meaning, and with the rose as a mandalic figure.

18

Annunciation and Incarnation

This sculptural series represents the angel that places their hands on Mary. Obviously, the incarnation is prior to the birth of the Baby Jesus, which shows that Gaudí did not follow a chronological order in the design of the façade.

The laying of hands implies transmission: of the pardon, of a blessing, of strength. In general, it is the transmission of a beneficial energy. It is a much-used technique in curing the sick. In fact, shaking hands is transmitting a tiny bit of positive energy. Holding hands is always a sign of peace and harmony.

In the symbolism of the human body, the hands are the main transformer or donator; they are the vehicle that the human being uses to change the reality that surrounds them. The hands represent the rational intervention of man in the world that surrounds him. It is also highly significant that there are two, since they represent the cosmic polarity, and that each one has five fingers, since five is the number of the human being, or rather, of the tendency towards perfection by the human being. Continuing with the symbolism of the hands, we can say that that the fact that the total number of fingers is ten also has a strong symbolic meaning, since ten is the number of unity (10511051). Joining or clasping the two hands and, therefore, overcoming the duality, leads us to unity, and unity is the principle, the central point of God. In some traditions they also speak of mystical or alchemical marriage.

Laying the hands on the head of a person is to invoke and transmit to them the gift of the Holy Spirit, for a mission or specific task. Therefore, it is highly logical and reasonable that the angel uses its hands for the incarnation of Mary.

Above the star that announces the birth of Jesus, Mary receives the angel of the Annunciation. The sculptural group is framed by a monumental rosary.

19

Signs of the Zodiac

Situated in the vaulting over the sculptural group of the Incarnation, are the first six signs of the Zodiac, from Aries to Virgo, that is, 180 degrees or half circumference. It might surprise one that Gaudí places the six first signs and forgets the other six, and why the first six and not the second six?

The fact is that if the period of gestation of the Baby Jesus was nine months, like any other human being, and his birth coincided with the winter solstice, the conception or incarnation must have been the 21st of March or spring equinox, when the astronomical year begins and, therefore, the astrological year. Thus, the incarnation coincided with the beginning of the astrological cycle. Why then did Gaudí not place three more signs and reach the nine months and the moment of the birth of the Baby Jesus? The answer is probably because he wanted to respect the sense of totality that the astrological representation has, of 360 degrees or full circumference, and wanted the half circumference to correspond to exactly six signs.

In any case, it is surprising to see the presence of astrological elements, because the Catholic Church has always been, and even more so in those years, a firm detractor of astrology, either adopting an allegedly scientific and rationalist point of view, or censuring it as a pagan practice. The coexistence of orthodox liturgical elements with the signs of the Zodiac is curious. Perhaps this is why the six representations of the Zodiac are rather vague and difficult to see clearly.

However, if a science or discipline studies the influence or confluence of the world above or the divine of the world here below or human world, it is astrology. And if all temples are or have been a meeting point between the ascending and descending forces, it is in some way logical and natural that in the Sagrada Família some role is awarded to astrology. The concern, independence and strict rigour of its architect shows it.

Representation of the sign of Gemini.

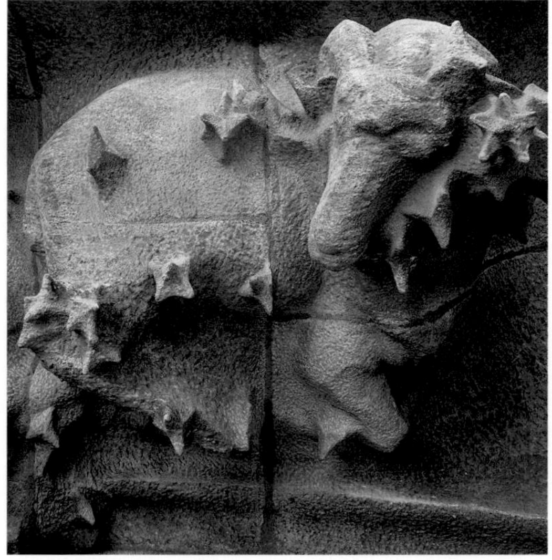

Representation of the sign of Aries, the first of the Zodiac.

Representation of the zodiacal sign of Taurus. The stars of the constellation emerge from the sculptural form.

General view of the zodiacal signs on the vaulting of the sculptural group of the Incarnation.

(Overleaf)
Group of angels that descend from Heaven singing the Sanctus Deus and Coronation of Mary, sculptural group by Llorenç Matamala.

Cathedral of Chartres
Zodiacal signs sculpted on one of the cathedral doorways.

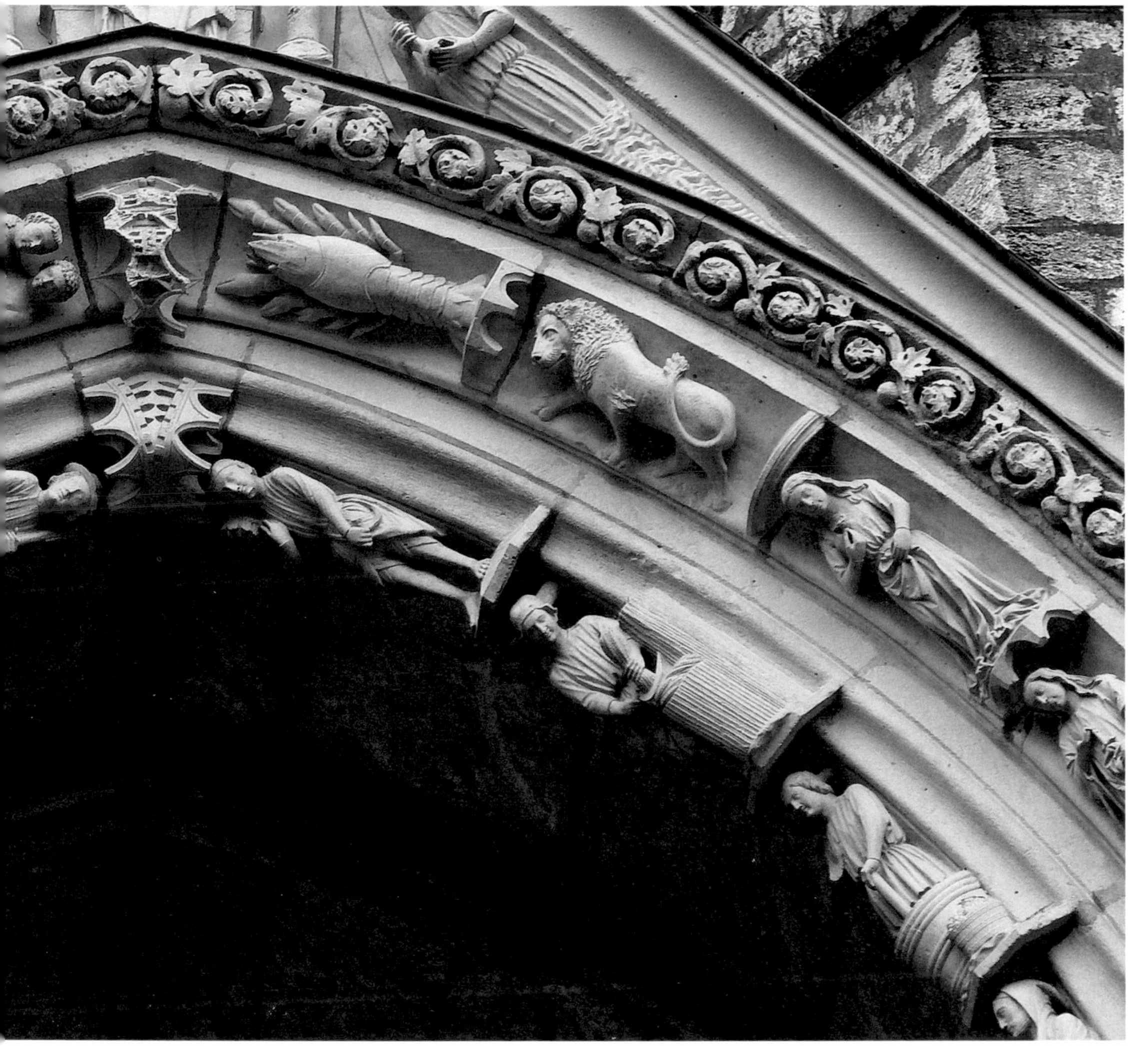

The Coronation of Mary

Situated in a central and preeminent spot of the façade, the composition of this sculptural group is rather unorthodox, or at least a little unusual, since Jesus, sitting on a throne, crowns the Virgin Mary. The figure of God the father is replaced by Saint Joseph (remember that the Temple of the Sagrada Família is dedicated to this saint) and the Holy Spirit is replaced by a third man placed in the background.

In this series by the sculptor Matamala, Gaudí wanted to place emphasis on the family and on filial veneration and love. It is God the son, alone, who crowns his mother, with his father among the men, Saint Joseph, as witness. This circumstance shows the importance and unity of the family and strengthens the love and recognition of mothers. God makes man crown his mother, turning her into a queen.

The icicles draw a type of triumphal arch that frames this scene. They symbolise the divine or higher influence, that from above, on the world here below. They strengthen the symbolism of the temple as a place of meeting and overlapping between the world beyond above and the world here below. The icicles, however, are rainwater or from above, in reserve, since ice is a reserve of water. Therefore, the scene is trimmed by a large reserve of water from the sky or a celestial source. Water is the basic and fundamental principle of life and fertility; it is the medium in which life has started. This symbolism of the starting of life links up perfectly with the function of motherhood, obviously befitting mothers. In this series, as on so many other occasions and circumstances, homage is paid to the maternal function through the Virgin, who becomes the synthesis of all mothers. In this way all mothers are crowned queens.

After this series there is a group of angels that descend while singing the *Sanctus Deus*. Some people have pointed out that these angels with their mouths open appear blind, without eyes. It is most likely that they had to be painted and that the eyes were obtained through this painting, which would change the expression on their faces dramatically.

Name of Jesus

Over the sculptural group of the Coronation of the Virgin we find an elaborate and spectacular anagram of Jesus (JHS). Monograms, above all those of the early Christians, are also the mandalas of Christianity, and as such, must be a direct way towards contemplative meditation. This monogram of Jesus was originally IHS, and represented the expression *in hoc signo* (with this sign), but in its present form, JHS (the I is now a J), it means *Jesus Hominum Salvator* (Jesus Saviour of Humanity).

The three letters representative of the name of Jesus Christ, JHS, are set or "crucified" over a Greek cross and flanked by the letters alpha and omega, which symbolise the beginning and end of all things. The cross is Greek because it is the one that best symbolises the conjunction of opposites in the earthly world. Of all the forms of cross, it is the most material, because it has four equal arms and therefore is centred on a circumference, and four is the number of the material world par excellence, four seasons, four cardinal points, four elements, etc.

In consequence, what appears between the alpha and the omega is the totality, the world or the cosmos in all its extension; in this case, the name of Jesus Christ. It has the same meaning as in the Apocalypse: "I am the Alpha and the Omega", declares Lord God, "the one who is, who was and who is coming, the Almighty". Jesus Christ is thus the beginning and end of all things. The fact that they have the mandalas as background and which are often inscribed in more or less clear circles, strengthens the symbolism of totality.

On the monogram of the Nativity Façade it advances the argument of the sacrifice of salvation that the death of Jesus Christ represents on the cross, a message that is global, between the alpha and the omega, and universal, that is to say, for the whole world: the sacrifice of Jesus Christ is for all humanity, without exception.

The pairs of angels surround the monogram, in some way related to the Eucharist. On the upper part, one carries a breadbasket and the other an amphora, which are the bread and the wine. The two in the middle are throwing incense with two censers, and the lower pair is collecting the blood of Jesus Christ to later sprinkle it around the world.

Alpha (higher) and omega (lower) from the anagram of Jesus surrounded by three pairs of angels (right).

JHS

Pelican

In reality, it is a family of pelicans, situated at the foot of the cypress and behind the egg. The pelican is an old symbol of Jesus Christ, because if the mother pelican is capable of living her life to save the lives of her young, Jesus Christ is capable of dying at the cross in order to save humanity. The mother pelican saves her chicks feeding them and giving them warmth with the fish and with the blood she has in her stomach, inasmuch as the blood of Jesus Christ on the cross serves to save or spiritually redeem humankind. The blood of Jesus Christ on the cross represented by the mother pelican is collected by the two angels placed on the sides, one with a jar, the other with a breadbasket.

However, the symbolic identification of the pelican with the sacrifice of Jesus Christ and, by extension, with altruistic love, is based on a mistake in the observation of the behaviour of adult pelicans. They do not open up the breast with the beak and make blood and fish sprout to give warmth and nourishment to their offspring: the only thing they do is empty their throat pouch in which they carry the fish they have caught to feed their chicks, just like other species of birds do to feed the chicks in their nests. This mistake of zoological observation does not invalidate, however, the symbolic content of the pelican.

National Library of France
Pelican, symbol of the sacrifice of Jesus Christ.

The egg

Red and yellow, it is situated at the foot of the cypress of the Nativity Façade. It has engraved on it the anagram of Jesus Christ, which we find a few metres below, JHS. The symbolism of the egg is directly related to that of birth, since the egg is the hidden source that contains the universe in the making.

The birth of the world from an egg is an image present in many cultures and traditions: it is the cosmic egg. In Catalan folklore, a curious form, *L'ou com balla* [the dancing egg], recalls the symbolism of the egg. On the day of Corpus Christi a previously emptied egg is placed over a jet of water; following its movements, the egg remains at the top of the jet of water, "dancing". We should remember that water is, symbolically, the birth of life.

The egg is a primordial or primary reality that contains in seed the great variety of beings existing in creation. The egg, however, also symbolises the source of spiritual life, that which refers to alchemical tradition when speaking of the philosophical egg.

The presence of an egg on the Nativity Façade is almost obligatory. The birth of a new man, or profound renovation, and immortality are two of the characteristics associated with the birth of the Messiah. The birth of the son of God is like a refounding or recreation of the universe in true and real life. This is forever, it is immortal. The message that Jesus Christ brought is a message of eternal renovation.

The pelican at the base of the cypress tree represents the Eucharist.

The egg at the feet of the pelican decorated with an anagram of Jesus, in red, symbolises life and resurrection.

24

The cypress and the doves

It is curious that in an outstanding spot of the Nativity Façade there is a cypress, a tree that today, due to its inevitable presence in many cemeteries, is associated with death. The symbolism of the cypress, however, more than being related to death, is related to time, to Kronos (Saturn), and in this sense is a symbol of long life, and more specifically, of eternal or spiritual life. The presence of the cypress in cemeteries therefore indicates that death does not mean no longer existing, but rather passing into eternal life.

The cypress is the tree of Life with a capital 'L' or, in other words, the tree of immortality. Not, however, a specific and particular immortality, but the immortality of the divine message, that of eternal life.

The birth of Jesus is the origin of Christianity and also the origin of a way of renewing this eternal message of spiritual life or great tradition. The message of Jesus Christ is a message of eternal time, a time outside time. The presence of the cypress on this façade is not, however, only down to the formal similarity to the towers of the Sagrada Familia, since the form is energy and a vertical and stylised form transmits an energy of elevation, transcendence, spiritual life: in short, growth.

The cypress is full of white doves. In the Christian tradition, the dove symbolises the Holy Spirit, the third member of the Holy Trinity. The white dove also represents purity and the soul. Nevertheless, the white dove of this façade is clearly the Holy Spirit present in the conception "by work and grace of the Holy Spirit" and which keeps watch over, from its privileged and high position, all the events prior to and immediately after the birth of the son of God. It thus undertakes the function of overseer and mediator between the divine plane and the earthly plane. The raised, privileged and central location on the Nativity Façade thus confirms it.

The symbolism of the cypress and that of the doves is mutually strengthening, since both refer to the supremacy or preponderance of the spiritual aspect.

25

The tau, the X and the dove

At the top of the cypress situated on the pinnacle of the Nativity Façade and which culminates the three doorways (Hope, Faith and Charity) there is a cross in the form of a tau (the tau is the first letter of the name of God in Greek), an X and several white doves. We have already seen that the cypress symbolises eternal life or the immortality of perennial tradition, the invisible thread that runs through the authentic traditions, schools, religions, etc. These three elements represent the three figures that make up the Holy Trinity, the Father, Son and Holy Spirit. The Father is the cross in the form of the tau, the Son is the X (chi) and the Holy Spirit is the dove.

If all crosses are, symbolically, the conjunction between two opponents or opposites, in this case the celestial world and the earthly world are represented by the vertical axis and horizontal axis, respectively. The cross in the form of T or tau strengthens this symbolism, emphasising the opposition between the two concepts. "The cross of the tau symbolises the snake nailed to a pole, death beaten by sacrifice". The snake, the earthly world or death are defeated by sacrifice or the celestial world.

The tau, the X and the dove, however, form a mystical cross, according to the terminology of the early Christians, which has a symbolic reading, along with the anagram of Jesus Christ that we find some metres below: "The seal is engraved with a cross in the form of tau (T); the chi (X) crosses the vertical line of the tau, which is rounded in the form of the rho (P). The name of Christ and the form of his cross is summarised in these lines. Christ, son of God, is the beginning and end of everything; the alpha and the omega, beginning and end of the intellectual signs and, by extension, of intelligence and the human soul, on both sides of the cross, right and left".

The cypress tree that crowns the Charity Doorway represents Eternal Life.

26

Ladders

At the foot of the central cypress there are two ladders with seven rungs. The symbolism of the ladder always refers to the relation between heaven and earth. The ladder is the symbol par excellence of the ascension, a gradual ascension that places in contact diverse levels in the two directions, ascension and descent. In many artistic representations it is the imaginary support of the spiritual ascension.

The symbolism of the ladder is identical to that of the tree in general: both refer to the ascent, to verticality, to the axis of the world, etc. This symbolism is specific when we speak of the tree of the world, the tree that allows transit between the two worlds. While the symbolism of the tree is close to the symbolism of the cross, the symbolism of the ladder also takes part in that of the cross.

Symbolically, all ladders have seven rungs or levels, since the passing from the earth to heaven requires crossing seven cosmic planes that are the seven planetary spheres, corresponding to the seven planets, the seven liberal arts, the seven works of charity, the seven basic colours, etc. Focusing more on the symbolism, they would be the seven angles of Jacob's ladder. The symbolism of the seven-rung ladder is a classic among the fathers of the Church and the mystics of the medieval period. We should also recall that seven is the number of the cycles par excellence.

On the pinnacle of the Nativity Façade we find three powerful symbols that are practically equivalent and which strengthen each other: from top to bottom, the two ladders, the cypress and the cross in the form of tau. They are three symbols that make a bridge and connect the earthly world here below with that of above, which make ascension and elevation possible for mankind. The ascent via the seven steps or rungs of the ladder enables us to reach the tree of life or immortality, and all thanks to the sacrifice of the coming of the son of God to the earth, represented by the cross in the form of tau. This reading synthesises the general symbolism of the whole façade.

27

Bridge

Between the two central towers of the façade (those of the Apostle Simon and the Apostle Jude Thaddeus) a bridge passes just beneath the upper part of the cypress. Symbolically, a bridge is always a nexus of union and communication between two realities. It is the universal symbol of the pass or transition from one state to another. In this sense, it is similar to the symbolism of the ladder or tree, which also represents the passing from one reality to another or from one plane to another, but in a vertical direction. The two ladders at the foot of the cypress and the cypress itself refer to the same symbolism, strengthened by the bridge. It is the passing from one reality to another, qualitatively different reality. The birth of the Son of God gives rise to, and is also a historic opportunity, the realisation of this change of state.

The title of Pontiff is etymologically linked to "bridge". It is significant that this title was given to Roman emperors, with continuity in giving the name to the Pope, because these pontiffs or bridge builders did not only make physical bridges that were used to cross rivers, but also built spiritual bridges, which were used to join heaven and earth, the plane of contingency with that of immortality, etc.; in short, they joined two qualitatively different realities. These pontiffs or public works engineers of today are both the constructors of the physical bridge and the span of the bridge, in that they work as mediators between the two realities.

I think that Gaudí also wanted to become a pontiff. Not only, however, through the construction of this narrow and high bridge on the façade. The very construction of the Expiatory Temple of the Sagrada Família is an act of mediation, befitting of a pontiff. The temple in itself is, through Gaudí's desire, a bridge between heaven and earth. The symbolism and structure of the inside of the temple strengthen this idea of interpenetration and communication between the two worlds. All temples —and clearly the Temple of the Sagrada Família as well— must be the meeting point between heaven and earth.

Comillas
Stained-glass window of the Pontifical Seminary that reproduces the coat of arms of Leon XIII, very similar with the cypress and the bridge to the Nativity Façade.

Drawing by Robert Fludd that symbolises the ascent from one plane of reality to another by means of a ladder.

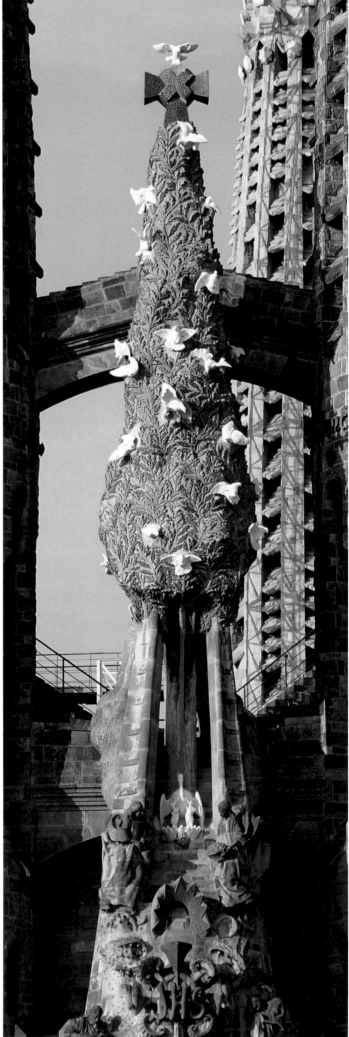

Birds

As flying animal, birds are the ideal symbol for relations between heaven and earth. They are therefore the messengers, and often also the perfect message, between the world there up above and the world here below. The bird is also the symbolic opposite to the snake; one is a symbol of the heavenly world, and the other, the earthly world.

The sacred literature of all religions and traditions is full of passages that refer to the symbolism of birds —the Upanishad, the Bible, the Koran, the *Mantiq al-Tayr* (The Language of Birds) by Farid al-Din `Attar or *Tale of the Birds* by Avicena. The language of birds —the way of flying, birdsong, etc.— has always been related to the divine language, the language of the gods. This is because this language refers to primordial purity, the hymn of creation. Therefore, it was almost obligatory that on the Nativity Façade of the son of God, with everything that re-foundation or recreation involves, there would be birds present.

The general symbolism of birds is related to the symbolism of the angels, also largely present on this façade. Both symbolise thought, imagination and the speed of relations with the spirit. However, if birds are symbolically the states of the spirit, angels are the higher states of being.

Winged animals symbolise the sublimation of the instincts and predomination of the spirit. It should be said that, apart from the general symbolism, each bird has its own symbolism, or rather, a symbolic specialisation within the general symbolism.

The culinary traditions befitting the Christmas day meal (chicken, turkey, rooster, etc.) refer to the symbolism of birds. If not, then why do all the traditional dishes on this day have wings?

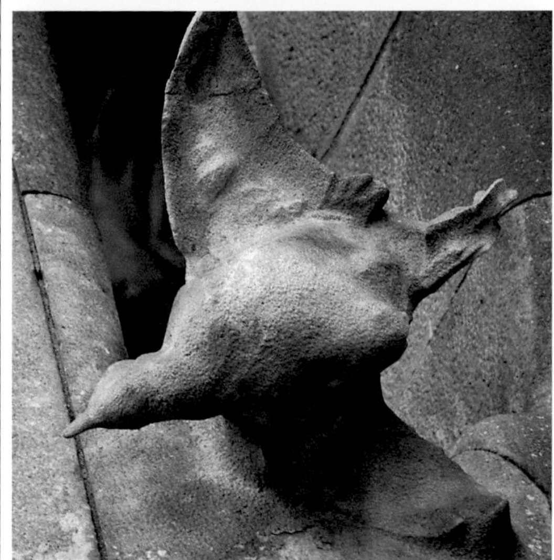

Birds of the Charity Doorway. The birds seem to come out of the stone flying in all directions.

Hope Doorway

Situated to the left of the Charity Doorway, it carries the anagram of Mary over a star, the Stella Maris that guides the boat steered by Saint Joseph. Its sculptural series depict the manifestations of this theological virtue: the marriage of Joseph and Mary and the images of Saint Joachim and Saint Anne signify the paths that God has chosen to undertake the redemption.

The flight to Egypt and the slaughter of the holy innocents are two of the most painful episodes in the childhood of Jesus Christ, these moments being when the virtue of hope is most necessary.

The two symbols on the upper part of the doorway are: the pinnacle relating to the Virgin —a crag of the mountain of Montserrat with the words *Salva nos* (save us)—, and in the lantern, the boat of the Church, skippered by Saint Joseph with the help of the Holy Spirit.

The flora of the cavities of the archivolt is aquatic, since the doorway recalls, in its totality, the stay of Jesus in the country of the Nile, Egypt: papyruses, lotuses, water lilies, pontederiaceae, thalias, bulrushes, eryngoes and vines with grapes. The fauna of the pedestal is also aquatic: geese, moorhens, etc.

29 The Holy Innocents
30 The marriage of the Virgin Mary
31 The Flight to Egypt
32 The wise man and the Baby Jesus
33 The saw and other tools
34 Saint Joseph on the boat

Details of the flora and fauna of the banks of the Nile.

Anagram of the Virgin.

34
30
32
31
33
29

Holy Innocents

The fauna and flora of the banks of the Nile that we find in this sculptural series, apart from referring to the region where the historic events took place, also has a symbolic content. The three birds, a species of duck or moorhen, take part in the symbolism of birds, but particularly concerning the soul.

Birds, however, also symbolise destiny, this higher force that determines the lives of individuals, not in a capricious way, but obeying a set of laws and a logic that is above the comprehension of mere mortals. We can say that the existence of the newborn children that Herod orders to be killed was totally conditioned by a powerful line of destiny: that which made their birth coincide with that of the son of God. Their life was cut short by this "coincidence" of destiny.

This group of newborn children were called by tradition "holy and innocents". The event in itself has been classified as sacrifice, and therefore, we are before the sacrifice of some holy innocents. If we lose sight of the total vision that destiny provides and stick to the strictly historical anecdote, we are before an event of sublime injustice. What fault did these poor children and their families have? Or, I do not understand why these things occur. It is the mother of the sculptural series who begs the executioner not to kill her son.

If, however, we broaden the vision and place ourselves in the setting of the coming of the Messiah and the birth of the son of God, we begin to understand, at least to place, that massive infanticide. We understand that one speaks of sacrifice and that the poor children are sanctified. A sacrifice has, in all cultures, two aspects: on the one hand it is the renunciation of earthly links —living life is the most dramatic earthly renunciation possible— and on the other hand, it is the recognition of divine supremacy. The communion of the saints, for Christians, is the maximum expression of the immortality of the soul.

The birds at the base of the figures represent the souls —immortal by definition— of those holy innocents. Destiny made the sacrifice of those newborn children, of those holy innocents, to make the life of the son of God possible, who was the carrier of the message of Christian revival on earth.

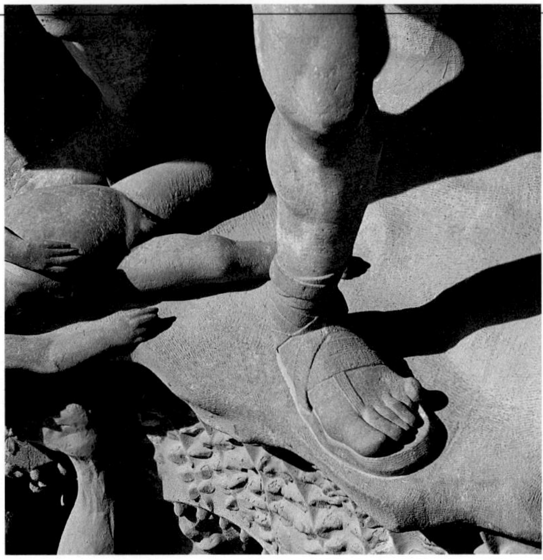

Details of the sculptural series of the Holy Saints; the Roman soldier's foot has six toes, as did the young assistant from whom the mould was taken and which Gaudí did not want to change. Work of Llorenç Matamala.

Betrothal of the Virgin Mary

Beyond the concept of marriage as the union through love of a man and a woman, and beyond that of the sacrament or the institution, all marriage is symbolically the overcoming of the duality of the manifest world, in order to achieve unity. In alchemy one speaks of alchemic marriages, being the conjunction reached with the union of sulphur and mercury, and it is also the union of the king and queen.

In the marriage of Mary and Joseph, the virginity of Mary symbolises the divine origin of life. In this case it is unquestionable, because it is about God becoming man. The Virgin Mary or divine mother is the soul in which God receives himself, since only He is. For God to be able to fertilise, however, the soul of the Virgin must be perfectly unified. According to the tradition, Mary married Joseph when she was twelve years old, before having menstruated. In this way, the purity of the Virgin is further emphasised. In mystical sense it means the union of Christ with the Church, of God with his people or of the soul with God.

In the foreground of this composition we find a bread basket with roses, the flower of love par excellence. The rose, however, is above all the flower of knowledge that is obtained through the heart, though love. It is intuitive knowledge, that which flows directly from the heart, without having to pass through the filter of reason.

In the marriage between Joseph and Mary the overcoming of the duality or polarity leads clearly to unity, to the beginning of everything, to God, since the "fruit" of this union is God made into man.

(Right page)
Marriage of the Virgin Mary at the top of the Hope Doorway, work of Llorenç Matamala (above) and sculptural series of the Flight to Egypt (below).

Flight to Egypt

According to the Gospel of Saint Matthew, in dreams an angel warned Saint Joseph, the head of the family, of the intentions of the governor Herod: "Arise and take the young child and his mother, and flee into Egypt, and be thou there until I tell thee: for Herod will seek the young child to destroy him". A divine messenger sends the orders to the Holy Family. Saint Joseph does not hesitate for a moment in complying with the angel's orders. This angel is, without the slightest doubt, the one in the sculptural series riding an ass.

The fact that it is a female ass is of importance. Jesus Christ will also ride a female ass on his triumphal entrance on Palm Sunday. If the male ass is, in general, a symbol of the most instinctive forces, even diabolical, in the myth of the false prophet Balaam the female ass embodies beneficial forces and in later interpretations the symbol is completely reversed. However, just like on Palm Sunday it is clearly the spirit that rides matter, here it is also the son of God that dominates and defeats the material world, represented by the female ass. The female ass also symbolises humility, peace and poverty, aspects that will accompany all the acts of the son of God. The flight to Egypt, then, is an opportunity to recall and relive these values.

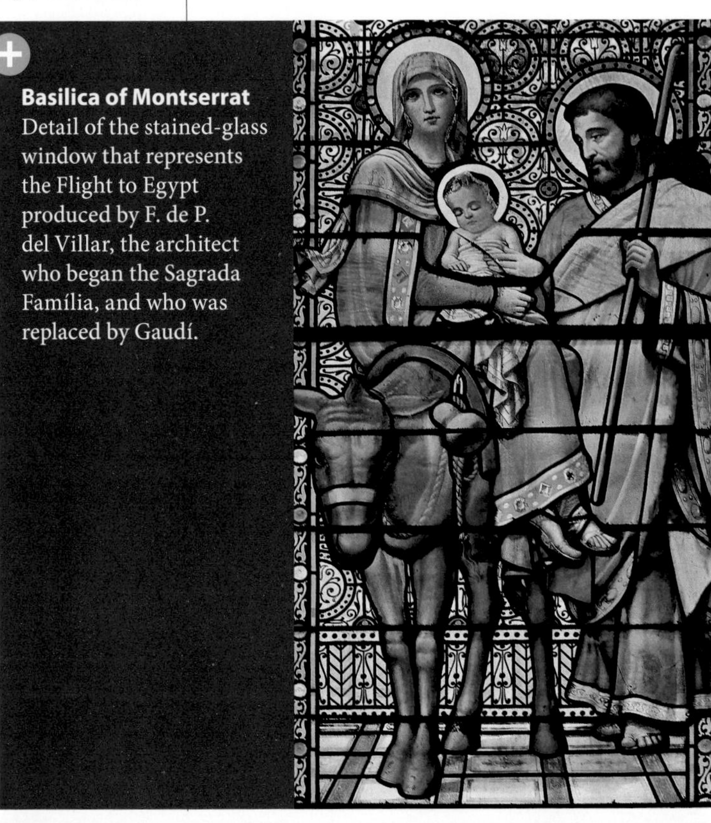

Basilica of Montserrat
Detail of the stained-glass window that represents the Flight to Egypt produced by F. de P. del Villar, the architect who began the Sagrada Família, and who was replaced by Gaudí.

30

31

Wise man and the Child Jesus

The dead dove that the Child Jesus carries is the symbol of simplicity and humility. When the Child Jesus surprisingly refutes the knowledge and teachings of the wise men of the temple, he does not wish to humiliate anyone or show off. The wise men of the temple are the representatives of science and established knowledge; they are the scholars and scientists of today, since in those times all knowledge was sacred. The Child Jesus only wants to transmit or communicate to them the message of renewal of which he is the carrier.

In current terminology, he is the representative of an alternative science that he brings to the representatives of official science. He does so very humbly, however, so as to avoid or minimise the rejection and disregard that will certainly be felt by official science. That a child or adolescent dares question the representatives of science, was and is even more so today, something clearly intolerable from the point of view of established scientists. I do not believe that it is going off on a tangent to state that the current universities are a clear example of what we have just said.

The opinions of the Child Jesus, however, do not seek confrontation or controversy, because they are not based on scholarly knowledge or from a new focus that brings a new school or current of thought to solve a problem. This would be the typical mechanism of inbred functioning that embodies the self-named scientific community. The knowledge of the Child Jesus comes from intuitive knowledge, superior to other forms of knowledge, since he is the son of cosmic knowledge, symbolised by the Akashic Records, the library of Alexandria or, in this case, the Holy Spirit. The clear connection of the Child Jesus with the Holy Spirit is what enables him to refute the opinions of the great wise men of the time. For this reason on the base of the figures of the Child Jesus and the wise man there is a dove with its wings open, which represents the Holy Spirit.

This sculptural series is framed in the upper part by diverse rosaries and the two figures of the maternal grandparents, Saint Joachim and Saint Anne.

Saint Anne and Saint Joachim, the young Jesus' grandparents, on the Hope Doorway.

(Right page) Sculptural series of the wise man and the young Jesus, who holds a dead dove in his hand.

33

Trunk saw and other tools

Below the sculptural composition of the Child Jesus and the wise man observed by his grandparents, Saint Joachim and Saint Anne, we come across the blade of large saw for cutting trunks, with the two handles at either end. Over the saw and framing the lower part of the sculptural group we find diverse tools belonging to different trades. Not all the tools are those of a carpenter, as it should be; they are, in fact, of trades relating to construction work. Actually, in the Gospel it does not say anywhere that Saint Joseph was a carpenter, but says he was a *tecnos*. The *tecnos* of the time came to be the builders or constructors of today, since they were the ones who built houses, both in stone and wood. The current mania for specialisation had not yet arrived. Gaudí must surely have loved this fact.

Among other tools, we find a mallet, a chisel, a set-square, a small shovel, a screwdriver, a hammer, an axe, etc. The school or tradition that has most developed the symbolic study of constructors' tools is the Masonry. We therefore see the symbolism of the constructors' most common tools.

The blow of the mallet on the chisel is the blow of the force of willpower, absolutely essential for intervening and transforming reality, and the chisel symbolises knowledge. Therefore, the force of willpower hits or pushes knowledge, in order to transform the world. The force of willpower without knowledge leads nowhere, and neither does knowledge without the force of willpower.

The set-square is the symbol of the upright behaviour that all humans need to control passions. The trowel, which is the tool with which the mixture or mortar is worked that joins the stones of a building, symbolises the fraternity that must exist between human beings.

Carpenter's tools on the Hope Doorway.

Saint Joseph on the boat

Saint Joseph, on a boat with a lantern, a clearly visible anchor and a baldachin on which the dove of the Holy Spirit has been placed, goes along a type of underground river beneath one of the Rocks of the mountain of Montserrat. The boat is the Church of Christ, steered by Saint Joseph, becoming its patron saint.

The symbolism of this boat, however, is not associated with the first symbolism of boat, that is, travel and crossing. The symbolism of this boat skippered by Saint Joseph is closer to the symbolism of the Ark, strengthened, on the other hand, by the baldachin in the form of an ark watched over or protected by the Holy Spirit.

The symbolism of the arch is linked to that of the egg of the world or renewal of cycle. A clear example is Noah's Ark. In Christian tradition the symbolism of the ark presents three aspects: (1) a new universal and eternal alliance; (2) a new and real presence, and (3) a new ark of salvation, but not from the flood —like that of father Noah— but from the sin of the world; in this sense the ark is the new Church and open to all, for eternal salvation. Therefore, what characterises this ark in the newness or renovation of the Church, through the coming of Jesus to the Earth.

The lantern that illuminates the crossing of the boat is the light that guides the path of the Church. Light is the universal symbol of knowledge, in contrast to darkness and confusion, which are symbols of ignorance. The lantern on the boat is the same as the lantern in the temples, the overhead opening through which light from the sky or the world above penetrates. Light, as well as being a symbol of knowledge, is also one of spirituality or nonmateriality. In this case, the light from the lantern is the light of spiritual knowledge, which guides the Church of Jesus.

Baldachin in the form of an arch protected by the Holy Spirit.

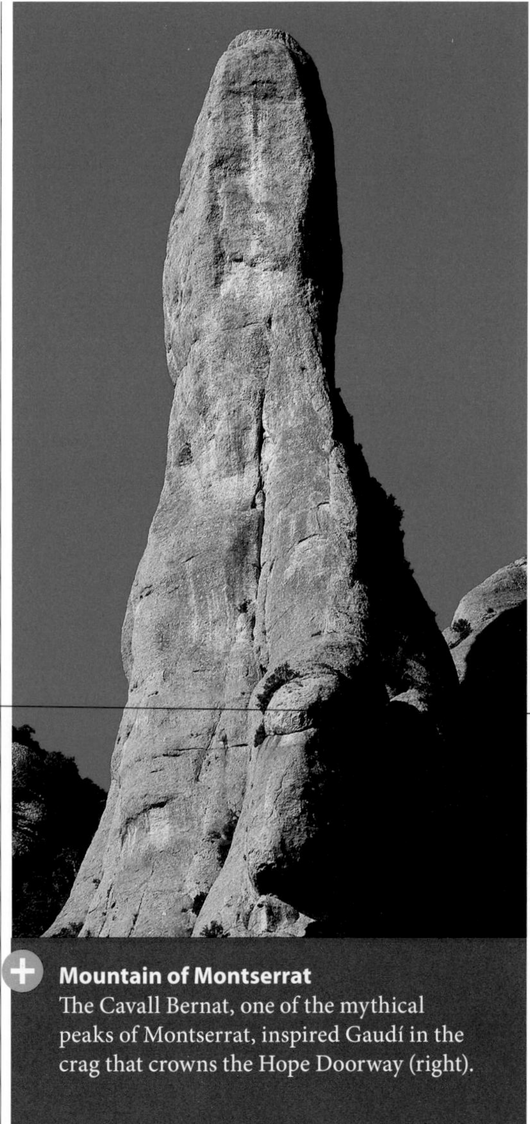

Mountain of Montserrat
The Cavall Bernat, one of the mythical peaks of Montserrat, inspired Gaudí in the crag that crowns the Hope Doorway (right).

Of the three symbolic meanings of water —source of life, means of purification or centre of regeneration—, we will settle for the latter, since the boat of Saint Joseph navigates through the underground waters of a cave. This regenerative symbolism of water would be strengthened if the upper rock is a rock from the mountain of Montserrat, by that of the Santa Cova.

The anchor is a symbol of solidity, stability and faithfulness, and is also the last hope remaining of the mariner in the midst of a storm. Remember that we are before the Hope Doorway of the Nativity Façade and, therefore, the anchor of the boat symbolises the solid and stable reference point for the Church of Jesus Christ. Saint Paul strengthens this symbolism when he says that we should anchor our souls in Jesus Christ to avoid the spiritual shipwreck. In the midst of the storm, into which human existence often becomes, the only solid and stable reference is the Church of Jesus Christ.

6

Faith Doorway

Situated to the right of the Charity Doorway, it carries the anagram of the patriarch Saint Joseph, since faith characterises the patriarchs.

The sculptural series of this doorway represents moments in the childhood of Jesus related to this theological virtue, such as the Visitation of the Virgin Mary, the revelation of the angel to Saint John, this latter announcing the coming of the Messiah or Jesus the child presented in the temple with the canticle of the priest Simeon. The central figure, over the lintel of the door, is the Child Jesus, aged 12, sitting on the faldstool while he explains to the doctors of Law the exact meaning of the Scriptures.

To the right we find Jesus helping his father Saint Joseph in the humble carpenter's workshop in Nazareth, surrounded by work tools, and also Joseph and Mary when they find Jesus in the temple.

The symbols of the pinnacle and of the lantern are logically related to the theological virtue of faith. The grapes and wheatears of the pinnacle are the symbols of the Eucharist. Another symbol refers to the Divine Providence. The Virgin Mary over the three-pointed crucible, in reference to the Holy Trinity, represents the dogma of the Immaculate Conception. On the lintel of the door there is a bleeding heart, in the wound of which mystical bees suck the nectar.

The archivolt of this doorway is full of exuberant vegetation, in this case, apples. However, also on this doorway we find violets, aloe and passionflower. The loggia that forms the lantern contains the group of the Presentation of Jesus in the temple, made up of Simeon and the Child Jesus and Mary prostrate on the floor.

35 The setting of Jesus preaching, the workshop of Nazareth and the Visitation
36 The Heart of Jesus
37 The Presentation of the Boy Jesus in the Temple
38 The Virgin
39 The lamp of the Holy Trinity
40 The bunches of grapes and wheatears
41 The palm leaves
42 The Providence

Cock beneath the sculptural group of the Visitation.

Anagram of the patriarch Saint Joseph.

40
42
38
39
40
37
41
35
35
36
35

35

Group of Jesus preaching, the Workshops in Nazareth and the Visitation

There are three sculptural series situated on the first level of the Faith Doorway. On the central part and in a higher position is the series of Jesus preaching in the temple, between the images of a young Saint John the Baptist and the priest Zacharias, son and father, respectively. On one of its sides, we find the episode of the Visitation of the Virgin Mary and her cousin Elisabeth, and on the other Jesus working as a carpenter in the workshop in Nazareth.

The nexus that links these three situations is strictly the chronological synchrony. In Gaudí's arrangement on the façade, however, one can see an interrelation between the three situations, since Joseph and Mary listen and admire Jesus preaching, from the level of the workshop in Nazareth. We can say that Gaudí is advancing the current technique of the comic, in which the situations interrelate from one drawing to another. It is as if a character breaks convention and moves into the next drawing.

In the vignette of Jesus preaching in the temple, the priest Zacharias, father of John the Baptist, is writing the name of John on the wall, when the angel announces to him that his wife is expecting.

In this series the situation or central and overwhelming vignette is that of Jesus preaching in the temple. The fact that it was Jesus doing it is explained by his importance in the Jewish religion.

(Right page and following) Set of scenes of the Faith Doorway: Visitation (B), Jesus preaching in the Temple (A) and Workshop of Nazareth (C).

A
C

A

C

B

Heart of Jesus

Just above the lintel of the entrance door is the heart of Jesus with thorns sticking in, bleeding. The heart is the organ or central point par excellence of all organisms and is associated with love, because the mystic union is the force that pushes towards unity, which is the centre. The mystic union can only be achieved through Love, with a capital "L", and the heart, the core and centre of the circumference are, symbolically, one and the same. In traditional cultures, the heart is also the organ of knowledge. Love and knowledge are situated in the same organ.

In Christianity the heart contains the Kingdom of God, the centre towards which the human being must return in their spiritual journey. It is the point where the divine activity that makes contact with the individual is situated, individuality, with a higher reality. It is what we call today the Inner Self. In a temple, the heart is situated in the altar.

The heart stabbed by thorns refers to the sacrifice of Jesus Christ to save humanity. It is the blood of Jesus Christ shed in his passion and death, and remembered every time the sacrifice is repeated at the Holy Mass, that which has redeemed and saved humanity. The heart is the organ of the human body that is basic and central to circulatory system, the system that circulates the blood and more closely linked to this, vital principle par excellence. In another order of things, the heart, with its two basic movements, systole and diastole, mark the profound and intrinsic rhythm of life.

In this heart of Jesus a bee sucks the blood. This animal is the symbol of industry and diligence, but in this context it becomes an emblem of Jesus Christ, because it has two sides: on one side is sweetness, and the other justice, inasmuch as Christ acts as judge.

Greek cross and heart of Jesus crowned with thorns in the Faith Doorway (above and right).

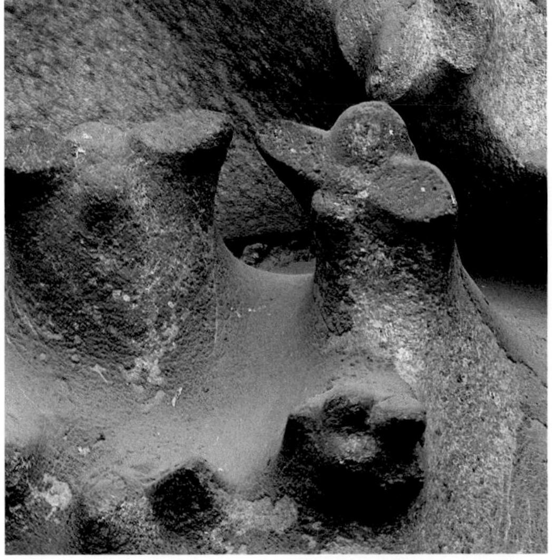

Details of the bees sucking the blood of Jesus.

Presentation of the Child Jesus in the temple

In compliance with Mosaic Law (the Law of Moses), which made it mandatory to present the first-born of all families to the temple, Joseph and Mary take Jesus there. Thus, the son of God is offered to God the Father in the Temple of Jerusalem.

The priest is Simeon, a just man, to whom the Holy Spirit had revealed that he would not die without having first seen the Messiah sent by God. Taking the child in his arms, Simeon thanks God for having been able to see the salvation of the people of Israel, while announcing to Mary the pain and suffering she will feel because of this.

This presentation includes the ritual purification of Mary, the mother. According to Mosaic Law, thirty-three days after the birth —prudent period of time to purify the blood— the woman had to make an offering in the temple and the priest made atonement for her, purifying her.

In this same scene we also find the prophetess Anne, who recognises the Messiah, the son of God, in Jesus, and she shows this to all those waiting for redemption.

Details of the sculptural scene of the Presentation of Jesus in the Temple (above) and sculptural group (right).

The Virgin

The doctrine of the Immaculate Conception certifies that Mary, mother of God, was saved from original sin from the moment she was conceived. This was possible due to the divine providence or preventive grace of Christ. The future role that Mary has reserved, to be the mother of God made into man, practically obliged her to be free of sin or blemish.

This belief, the result of popular sympathy, took several centuries to be accepted officially. Given that it is a belief without explicit biblical foundation, it became a recurring topic in theological discussions. The discussions were prolonged for practically ten centuries, and involved in them were great theologians and fathers of the Church. Saint Bernard of Clairaux, Saint Albert the Great, Saint Bonaventure and Saint Thomas of Aquino himself opposed the doctrine of the Immaculate Conception, based on the universality of the original sin, according to which not even Mary was exempt from. In contrast, it was defended by Ramon Llull and Duns Escoto. This theological dispute was also a traditional element of conflict between the order of the Dominicans —against— and that of the Franciscans —for.

The festival on the 8th of December that celebrates this belief was spread in the 9th century from the South of France towards England. It was accepted by Rome in 1476 and received the current solemnity after the dogmatic definition of Pius IX, in 1854.

This long dispute shows the need to highlight the exceptional and unique nature of the Virgin Mary, since it had to be in her where the son of God became incarnate, became man.

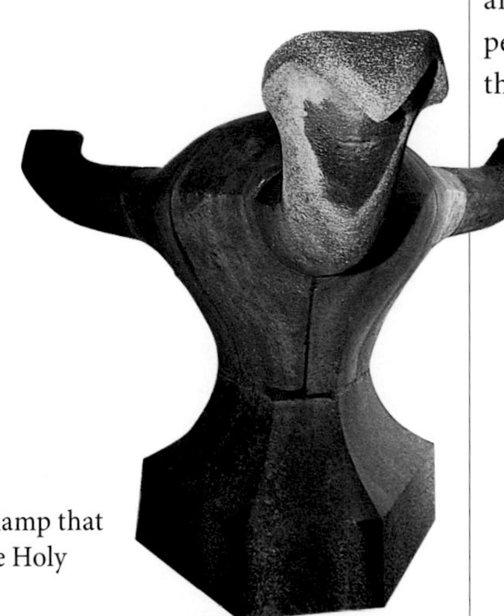

Three-armed lamp that symbolises the Holy Trinity.

The lantern of the Holy Trinity

This lantern represents the Holy Trinity because it has three holes. The Holy Trinity is three manifestations or representations of the same divine reality. Father, Son and Holy Spirit represent the operations of power, intelligence and love, which correspond, respectively, to the throne (the Father), the book (the Son) and the dove (the Holy Spirit).

In nearly all traditions or religions there are ternary series corresponding to aspects of the supreme God. They are like different sides or potentialities of God. The Holy Spirit, however, does not correspond to the ternaries or triads of Gnostic origin, in which the opposition between two elements produces the third; a classic and universal example of this type of triad is the father, mother and son. The Holy Spirit is three manifestations of the same reality, the divine reality. The three elements represent the three main manifestations of divine strength.

All lanterns are linked to the symbolism of light. Light is, to start with, knowledge and wisdom. However, the symbolism of the lantern or light is very rich. The transmission of the fire of the lantern is the symbol of the transmission chain of knowledge, a great tradition or perennial philosophy, which has existed since the beginning of time. The lantern also symbolises the real presence of God, and in another order of symbols, the fame represents the continuity of life. When a new life begins, a flame lights up, when a life is extinguished, a flame dies. The lantern is also the representation of the human being: the ceramic recipient is the body, the oil, the beginning of life, and the flame, the spirit.

The lantern with three holes represents the Holy Trinity, but also the Son of God made into man and forming part of an eternal tradition, called perennial tradition , a tradition that is an invisible thread, but more real than any reality.

The figure of the Virgin treads on the snake supported over the three-armed lamp and is surrounded by wheatears and vines as symbols of fertility.

Grapes and wheatears

The Eucharist is represented by the wheatears and the grapes, the bread and wine of eternal life, which can only be a donation of the gods. As is known, bread is the symbol of essential food and therefore of spiritual food, the sacred bread of eternal life.

Traditionally, the bread of the Eucharist has been linked to the active principle, inasmuch as wine has been related to contemplative life.
Bread symbolises the minor mysteries, and wine, the major mysteries. This aspect is clearly reflected in the two miracles of Jesus Christ: the miracle of the loaves is strictly quantitative, but the miracle of the wine at the wedding of Canaan is qualitative.

In the context of the Nativity Façade, the bunch of grapes is a symbol of fertility and the wine that is made from them is also a symbol of eternal life and sacred rapture. However, before the grapes and the wine, logically it was the vine, a sacred tree. We should not forget that in some traditions of the early Christians it was said that the tree of life of Paradise on earth was the vine. The vine is, therefore, symbol of life, and the wine, image of the initiation and knowledge. It is no coincidence that the father Noah, clear initiator of a new cycle, was the first to plant a vine.

In the Eucharist, instituted by Jesus Christ, the bread is the flesh and the wine the blood. Its celebration at mass is the repetition of a sacrifice, in which the sacrificial element has been symbolically replaced by the bread and wine. This replacement, however, does not diminish the intensity of the sacrifice, since when one eats the bread and drinks the wine, when receiving communion, one receives the food of eternal life.

Palm leaves

The palm leaves or green branches —symbolically they are the same— which are at the top of the two columns of the central Charity Doorway, have been in many cultures a symbol of victory and immortality, which is also a form of victory over death. Forming part of this symbolism is the golden branch of the mysteries of Eleusis, the branch of acacia of the Masonry or the mistletoe of the Druids.

The dried crafted palm leaves of Palm Sunday to which these palm leaves on the Nativity Façade refer to announce the resurrection of Jesus Christ after his Passion, Calvary and Death, since his resurrection is the realisation of immortality that also expresses his victory over death.

The image of a saint with a palm shows us that it is a martyred saint. The palms that martyred saints carry refer to this same symbol, to the victory that represents the immortality of the soul. It is not, however, a victory understood in the sense that, "although you torture and kill me, I am more powerful than you and I rise from the dead", it is an inner victory, over sin, sustained in love, which, on the other hand, is the eternal and definitive victory.

Bunches of grapes and palm leaves on the Faith Doorway.

40

41

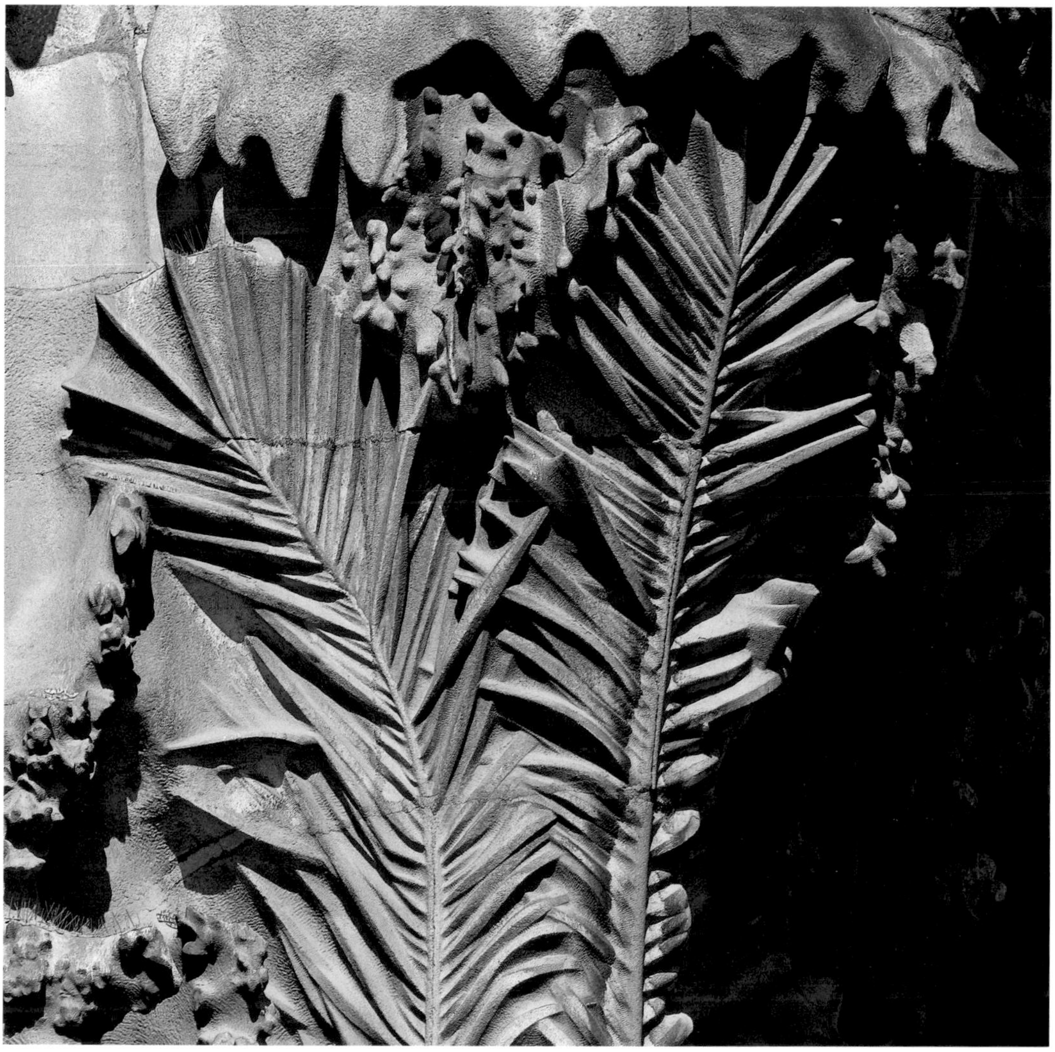

The Providence

The Divine Providence is represented by an eye framed in an extended human right hand. The hand-eye association symbolised "far-sighted action". All heterotopic eyes, that is, displaced from their natural position towards another part of the body, refer to the spiritual correspondence of vision: far-sightedness or clear vision.

It is the hand that guides and the eye that sees all. In fact, the providence is God's care of the transformation of the world and, especially, of the existence of man. In reality, it is God's project or planning for the cosmos and humanity and what the human being is unable to comprehend.

The hand symbolises the guiding or directing of the universe by God, and the eye, the higher knowledge that only God may have, the "God sees all" and, in consequence, knows all. It is not, then, feeling one's way along without direction, but a guiding that follows a careful planning: the divine providence.

However, the hand has been compared to the eye. The hands of men are linked to knowledge, to vision, since its finality is language. Classical psychoanalysis recovers this symbolism when it says that the hand that appears in a dream is equivalent to an eye. In some ways they are two symbols that strengthen and complete each other. They are action and knowledge.

Representation of the Divine Providence (above); wheatears of the pinnacle (below) and set of the crowning of the Faith Doorway (right).

Passion Façade

"If I had begun building this façade, people would have withdrawn, (...) that of the Death is hard, naked, as if made of bones."

Antoni Gaudí

While the Nativity Façade expresses life and exuberance, the Passion Façade, acording to Gaudí, transmits drama and cruelty. "Maybe some people find this façade too extravagant; but I would like it to even frighten people, and to achieve that I will not skimp on the chiaroscuro, the projecting and inset elements, everything that is more gloomily sensationalist."

One of the most impressive aspects of this façade is the atrium with columns that recall bones. The skeletal and anatomic forms structured in very simple geometric forms give it an air of eternal rest and stability. The sculptor Josep Maria Subirachs presents the Passion of Jesus Christ, from the Last Supper to the Crucifixion, in various settings and on a type of stage at three levels, free of all ornamentation in order to aid concentration of the spirit. The settings are read following the form of a reversed "S", that is, from left to right going upwards, in the chronological order in which they occurred.

The four bell towers are dedicated to Saint James, Saint Bartholomew, Saint Thomas and Saint Philip. Like the Nativity Façade, it has three doorways dedicated to theological virtues, Faith, Hope and Charity, situated beneath a support of five arches covered by a full-width gallery, which represents the states of limbo.

In the culmination of the windows we come across Mediterranean fruits from autumn-winter: chestnuts, pomegranates and oranges. Remember that this is the façade of Death, facing west, that is, the death of the sun.

The Passion Façade, however, as well as being the façade of pain and death, is also the façade of hope and resurrection. In initiation meaning, death comes prior to and is indispensable to resurrection. Clearly, so that the new man can be born, the old one must die first. In order to fill a recipient, first one must empty it.

The passion and death represented on this façade is a great initiation ritual, which Jesus Christ, the son of God, undertakes on behalf of all humanity. Jesus Christ becomes Man incarnate —with a capital "M"— and experiences the initiation ritual in representation of this universal man. It is as if the whole of humanity had gone through this ritual through Jesus Christ. The passion and death of Jesus Christ is, therefore, a collective initiation ritual of all humanity.

2 Passion Façade

43 Charity Doorway
44 Hope Doorway
45 Faith Doorway
46 The Last Supper
47 Malchus's ear
48 The magic square
49 The betrayal of Judas
50 The flagellation
51 The alpha-omega
52 The denials of Peter
53 The labyrinth
54 The crown of thorns
55 Jesus before Pontius Pilate
56 Way of the Calvary
57 The Veronica
58 Longinus
59 Playing for the robes
60 The crucifixion
61 The sepulchre
62 The burial

Hosanna
Excelsis
Sanctus

43

Charity Doorway

All the scenes from the Passion that take place inside buildings are arranged within niches, and those that take place in the open air are placed on pedestals. The most outstanding figure is that of Christ, with the word *Veritas* on the upper part. To one side, the women saints of Jerusalem, Longinus, Joseph of Arimathea and the disciples; on the other side are represented the blasphemers, the tormentors, the soldiers that mock Christ.

At a higher level (still to be built), Jesus Christ washes the feet of his disciples and leaves them the new commandment of love. Higher up, the word *Vita* points out the institution of the Eucharist in the Last Supper. Practically on the side of the tympanum, we find Christ alone against the light in the evening in the orchard of Gethsemane.

The pediment (still under construction) is a representation of the "Yes, Lord" of Abraham, in which the patriarchs and the prophets await the liberation that represents the coming of the Messiah, and specifically his passion and death, which counteracts the original sin. This is why the acroterium of the pediment are two biblical prefigurations of Jesus: the lion of Judas, which through its own strength defeats death, and the lamb trapped in the bramble from the sacrifice of Isaac who without a groan escapes from the sacrifice. The cross that tops the pediment has no image, and is the cross adored by the angels.

In the setting of the resurrection is the representation of the empty sepulchre, with the guardian angel, Mary Magdalene and Mary Salome. The image of Jesus resurrected is found on the large window of the transept, in which the figure of the ascension of Jesus, surrounded by angels, is found half way up the bell towers.

In between the end columns of the façade, within the latticed galleries, are represented the meetings of the priests and Pharisees of the village, in which the death of Jesus Christ is recalled. The pediment is a rampant gallery of nine small columns on each side that support a cornice on which one can read *Jesus Nazarenus, rex Judeorum.*

The door of the Gospel

In all traditions the book of revelation is by extension manifestation. The evangelical texts that we find on this door of two panels are, without the slightest doubt, the revelation that the son of God made man left behind; the two door panels strengthen the identification with an open book.

On assimilating the leaves of the book shown with the door panels of the entrance to the temple, it very clearly shows the symbolic and therefore real function of the gospels and the temple. Symbolically, entering the temple and reading the holy texts becomes the same act.

Ascension of Jesus (above) and Gospel doorway (below and following).

Sanctus San

JESUS D NATZARET REI DELS JUEUS
QUE ES LA VERITAT

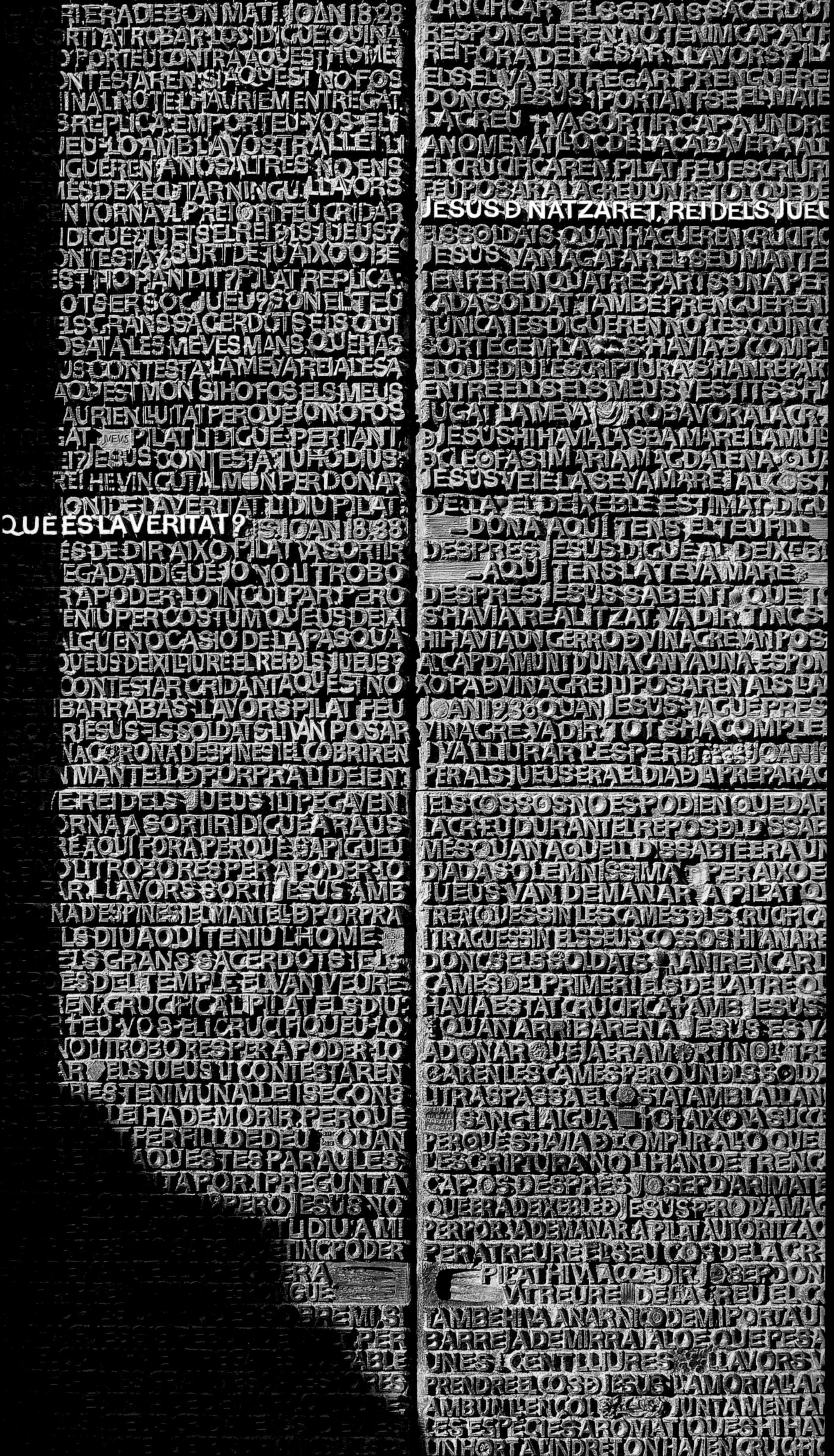
JESÚS D NATZARET, REI DELS JUEU
QUÈ ÉS LA VERITAT?

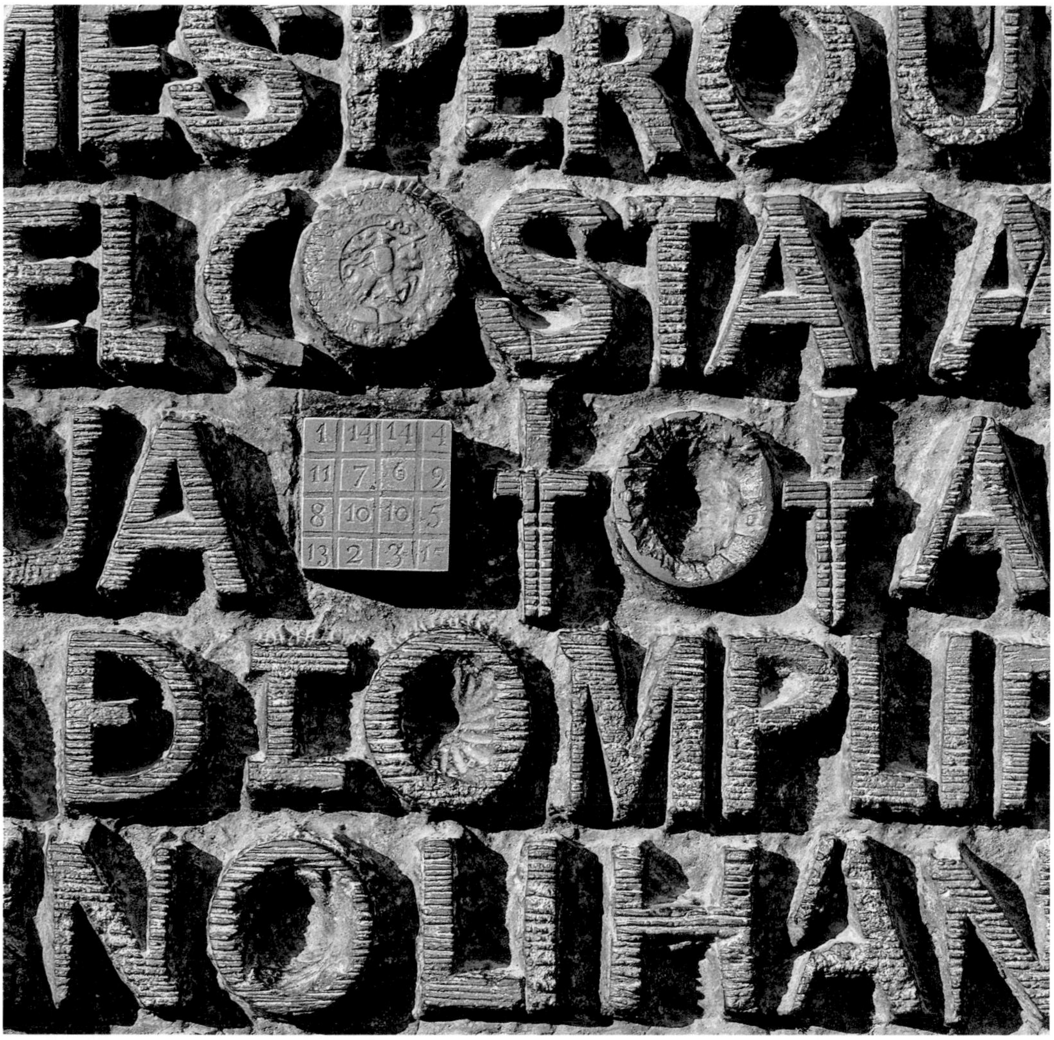
MESPEROU
ELC STATA
UA TOTA
1 14 14 4
11 7 6 9
8 10 10 5
13 2 3 15
DIOMPLI
NOLIHAN

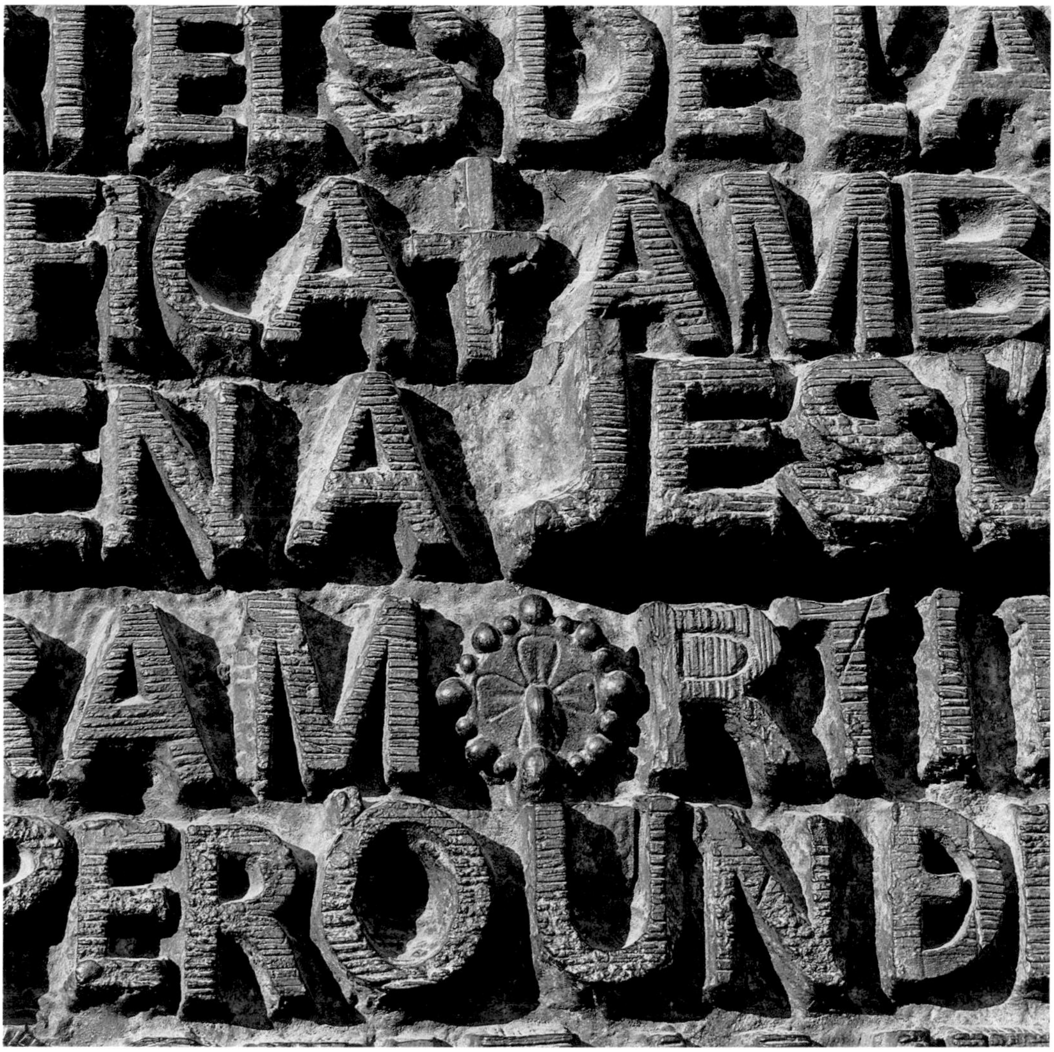
ELS DE LA
FICAT AMB
ENA ESU
AM RTI
PEROUND

44

Faith Doorway

The settings of this doorway are: the triumphal entrance of Jesus of Nazareth into Jerusalem; the appearance of Sanhedrin; before Caiaphus and when a servant beats him; before the council and before Herod, who mocks him by dressing him in white because he has not wanted to answer his questions.

Gethsemane doorway

Dedicated to the prayer of the garden of Gethsemane. So that there is no margin left for doubt, Subirachs has written the reference of the paragraphs of the Gospel according to Saint Matthew in which this scene is explained. After the Last Supper and after Jesus Christ announces to Peter and the other disciples that he will make three denials before the cock crows, they reach the garden Gethsemane.

It is here where Jesus Christ prepares for the events —prison, trial, Calvary, etc.— which will culminate in death on the cross. Before beginning the passion and death, Jesus Christ speaks with God the Father, praying. We believe that the most delicate, committed and important aspect of his entire mission on earth is about to begin. After instituting the Eucharist, only the passion, sacrifice and death on the cross remain. They are the moments prior to any transcendental event, and never better described. Jesus Christ goes to pray in the garden of Gethsemane.

His disciples, however, are not aware of the master's preparations, in short, of the decisive moments that they are living, and "they remain sleeping". When Matthew tells us, however, that after praying Jesus Christ finds them asleep, it is not that the disciples have slept little and are tired or that they have eaten and even drunk too much and must sleep it off, as some have clumsily interpreted; what is being said is that they do not realise what they are experiencing and are about to experience. They are "asleep" before all that is happening to them.

It is a very common symbol to say that someone "is sleeping" when they are not aware of or do not realise what is happening. This is precisely what occurred to the disciples of Jesus Christ, when Judas arrives and kisses him, beginning the whole process and the disciples, in an incipient way, begin to be aware of what is going on around them.

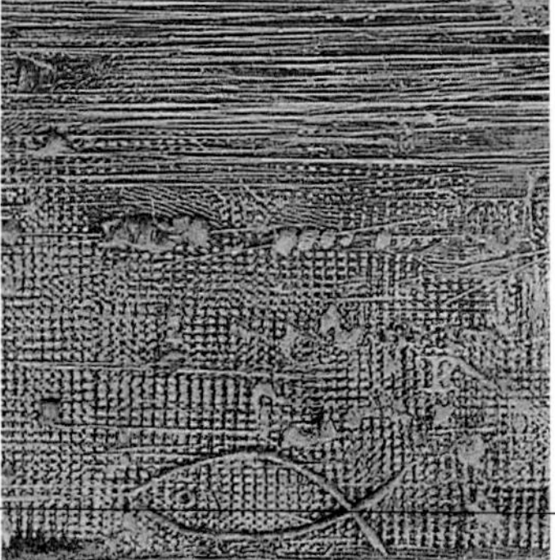

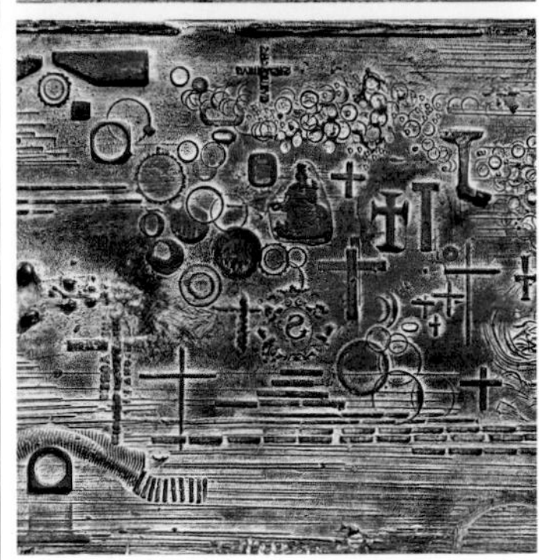

Sanctus
SEMANÍ
S ES DEIXÀ CAURE DE CARA A TERRA
EGAVA: PARE MEU, SI ÉS POSSIBLE,
PASSI LLUNY DE MI AQUEST CALZE
Ò QUE ES FACI
COM JO VULL,
Ò COM VOLEU VÓS, LLAVORS VA
EU 26,39

Hope Doorway

It brings together the most painful moments of the Passion: the scenes of the Praetorian Guard, the flagellation, the crown of thorns, the death sentence and the way of the Calvary. If the Faith Doorway is the triumphant "way", the Hope Doorway is the painful "way".

Coronation door

In the upper part of the bronze door of the Hope Doorway we can see Christ with the crown of thorns, the purple cape and the reed serving as royal sceptre. The crown, the purple cape and the sceptre are three clear symbolic elements and representative of power. Specifically, the power of kings.

These elements that are representative of royal power are used here as elements of mockery. The crown is not of gold, but thorns. The sceptre is also not gold, or of fine wood with incrustations of precious stones, but is a reed. Beyond the mockery, this man who it was said was the king of the Jews and as such was dressed in the attributes befitting his rank, works as a parody, and is a clownish representation of the coronation of a king.

Beyond the torture and the jibing, these elements contain a symbolic weight that gives them their own place and meaning in the symbolism of the passion and death of Jesus Christ. As can be seen if we look more carefully at the section of the crown of thorns, it is a symbol of divine immortality.

The cape, like all items of circular clothing open with a hole in the upper part, in the style of a chasuble, short cloak or chlamys, evokes the sheet —remember that the etymology of chasuble is "small house"— with a round central opening that, as well as serving as a chimney, is the ascending way or path. The priest dressed in the rain cape or chasuble finds himself ritually situated in the centre of the universe, constituted as the axis of the world. The cape is the celestial cabin and on the head, which is situated on a higher level, we find God, who the priest represents on earth. What better representation is there of God on earth than his own son? What better prototype of the Christian priest is there than Jesus Christ himself?

The sceptre corroborates and broadens the symbolism of the crown and the cape, since it is a reduced version of the large command staff. As a symbol, it is a pure vertical upright, which places Man with a capital "M" in contact with God. It is the favourite symbol of the King of the World. Therefore, these elements transcend their strictest sense of insult and mockery, and become first-class symbolic elements.

On the lower part of the door Jesus is taken before Annas and Caiaphas and confirms his previous declarations.

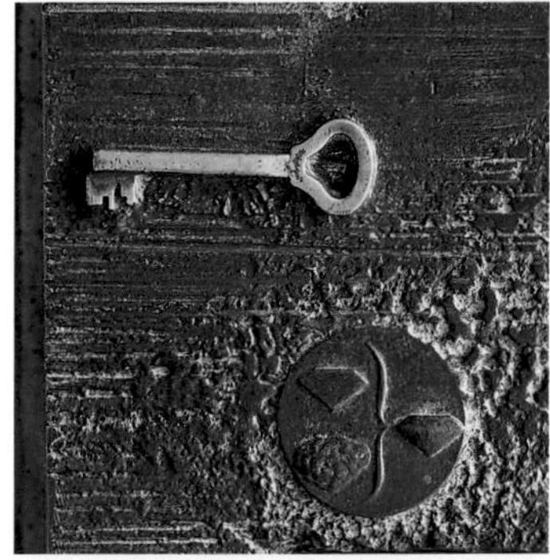

SOLDATS VAN TEIXIR
NA CORONA D'ESPINES
AHI POSAREN AL CAP
EL REVESTIREN D'UN
MANTELL DE PORPRA,
LI DEIEN: SALVE REI
DELS JUEUS! I LI PEGAVEN
BUFETADES
INRI
ECCE HOMO
A VEGADES ÉS NECESSARI I FORÇÓS
QUE UN HOME MORI PER UN POBLE,
PERÒ MAI NO HA DE MORIR TOT UN POBLE
PER UN HOME SOL:
RECORDA SEMPRE AIXÒ, SEPHARAD.
LLIBERTAT.
SALVADOR ESPRIU
IL MIO DISIR DEE AVER FINE
N QUESTO MIRO E ANGELICO TEMPLO
HE SOLO AMORE E LUCE HA PER CONFINE
PARADISO XXVIII 52-54
SUBIRACHS

The sculptures and doors of this façade are work of the sculptor Josep Maria Subirachs.

The scenes are read following the form of an "S" drawn from bottom to top.

46 The Last Supper

47 Malchus's ear

48 The magic square

49 The betrayal of Judas

50 The flagellation

51 The alpha-omega

52 The denials of Peter
53 The labyrinth
54 The crown of thorns
55 Jesus before Pilate
56 Way of the Calvary
57 The Veronica
58 Longinus
59 Playing for the robes
60 The crucifixion
61 The sepulchre
62 The burial

Last Supper

It is the sculptural series which starts from the narrative thread of this façade, which follows the outline of a backward S. Jesus Christ is facing his disciples and with his back to the observer, as if he wanted to emphasise the importance of the twelve apostles.

The Last Supper is the founding moment of the ritual of the Holy Mass and the establishment of the Eucharist. In this sense, it is a ritual of sacrifice that is repeated each time a mass is held; it is a ritual of red magic, because blood, almost always of an animal, is the fundamental aspect of the ritual. The Old Testament is full of these examples. According to the Hebrew religion, some acts may be redeemed through the blood sacrifice of the expiatory victim. On the same lines, the Arab refrain, "the blood has flown, the danger has passed", expresses very well the finality of all sacrifices: pacify the powers and keep misfortunes at bay.

The Holy Mass is a sacrifice of red magic, in which the wine is the symbolic representation of the blood of Christ. The Last Supper was, then, a founding ritual, a "pact of blood" that Jesus Christ —who knew he was going to die— wanted to establish with his disciples. To seal this pact, Jesus gave them his blood to drink; because according to ritualistic or analogical reasoning what the apostles drank was not wine, it was really Christ's blood. Once this central sacrament was established, all the events begin to develop, following step by step the script written by divine providence.

The dog placed in a corner on the right symbolises in the first instance loyalty, the loyalty of the disciples to the master. Nevertheless, in Christianity the dog is also a sheepdog, that watches over and guides the flock, which is the people of Christ. In this sense, the function of the dog is assimilated into that of the priesthood. We must not forget that the first priests of Christianity were the apostles. Going further into the deepest symbolism, the dog, like the vulture, accompanies the dead on their journey to resurrection. We should remember that the Last Supper marks the beginning of the passion of Jesus Christ, which ends with the resurrection from the dead.

Detail of the face of Jesus.

The apostle Judas hiding the coins of the betrayal.

The apostle John rests his head on the table exhausted.

Malchus's ear

The episode of the cutting of Malchus's ear by the apostle Peter in the olive grove has always been taken as a hymn to pacifism and the uselessness of the use of violence, which solves nothing and only produces more violence. We should recall that Jesus corrects Peter's crime, returning the ear of the server of the High Pontiff to its place; and here nothing has happened.

In this context, however, the ear is a symbol of obedience to the divine word. This is because it is through the ear that the disciples hear that they must understand and accept the divine message. In the whole episode of the arrest of Jesus, his disciples wander around a bit confused. For example, the fact of staying asleep while Jesus prayed is not related to the fact that they had slept little and were tired, but symbolises their incomprehension of the importance of the situation, their "being asleep" to that new reality announced by the son of God. Peter's action shows the little understanding they had at the time of the events they were playing a leading role in. In their favour we should say that it was not easy for those humble apostles to appreciate the moment they were living in.

The superposition of Malchus's ear with the section of a cut olive tree trunk is, I think, a good visual discovery. Since the ear symbolises comprehension, the olive is the symbol —in the Hebrew context— of the alliance between Jehovah and man. Despite the little understanding of the disciples, the message of eternal life reappears on the trunk of the olive, a tree that never dies. In this sense we should remember that the branch that the dove carried that announced to Noah the rebirth of life, was an olive branch.

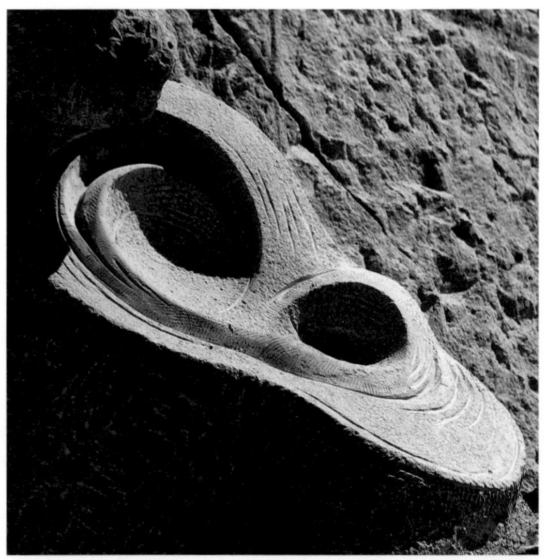

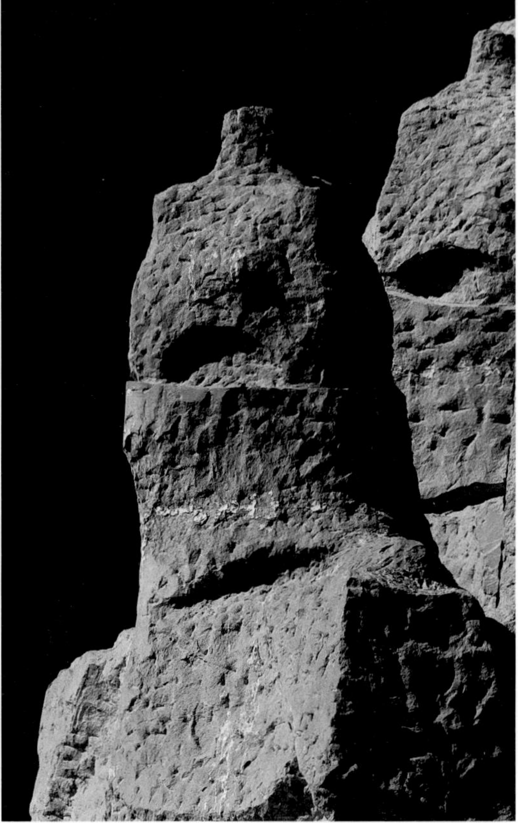

Detail of Malchus's ear (above) and of the soldiers' helmets (below).

Magic square

The basis of numerical cryptograms, also called magic stamps, is the consideration that every number communicates or transmits its own energy. For example, the energy and symbolism of the number 1 is not the same as that of the number 4. Just like colours or musical notes are the same vibration on a different wavelength, the different numbers are also representations of different vibratory waves. As is known, there is a close correspondence between numbers, letters, colours, musical notes, etc. Numerology and all the schools that derive from it, the cabala and others, are based on this reality. Pythagoras himself said that the cosmos could be represented numerically in its totality.

The numerical cryptogram on the Faith Doorway of the Passion Façade, situated in the sculptural series of the Kiss of Judas is of 4 × 4, 16 squares. It is known under the name of the Seal of Jupiter or the Numbers of God. While the odd squares such as that of 333 have a central cross, the even squares like this one has a central space. With these sixteen numbers one can make three-hundred and ten combinations of additions that always come to 33, the symbolic age of Jesus Christ when he died. The fact that the square is that of the age that tradition says Jesus Christ was when he died, strengthens the idea that this age has a strong symbolic content, as 33 is a number with a deep and powerful symbolism. The symbolic perspective rejects pseudo-historicist and literal interpretations, and consequently out of place, that attempt to demonstrate that when the son of God made man died he was not this age. The symbolic content of 33 is situated on a higher plane to that of the contingent anecdote of the age of death of Jesus Christ.

Magic squares, present in many cultures, traditions and religions, carry a secret meaning and a hidden power, since the square is the ideal means to capture and move energy that all numbers contain naturally. In this sense, magic squares have been used basically as protective amulets. The tradition that has most developed magic squares is Islam. There are squares in all the possible combinations; in fact, dealing with numerical combinations, it could not be any other way.

Durer
"Melancholy", where one can see a magic square over the head of the angel.

Numerical cryptogram based on the number 33.

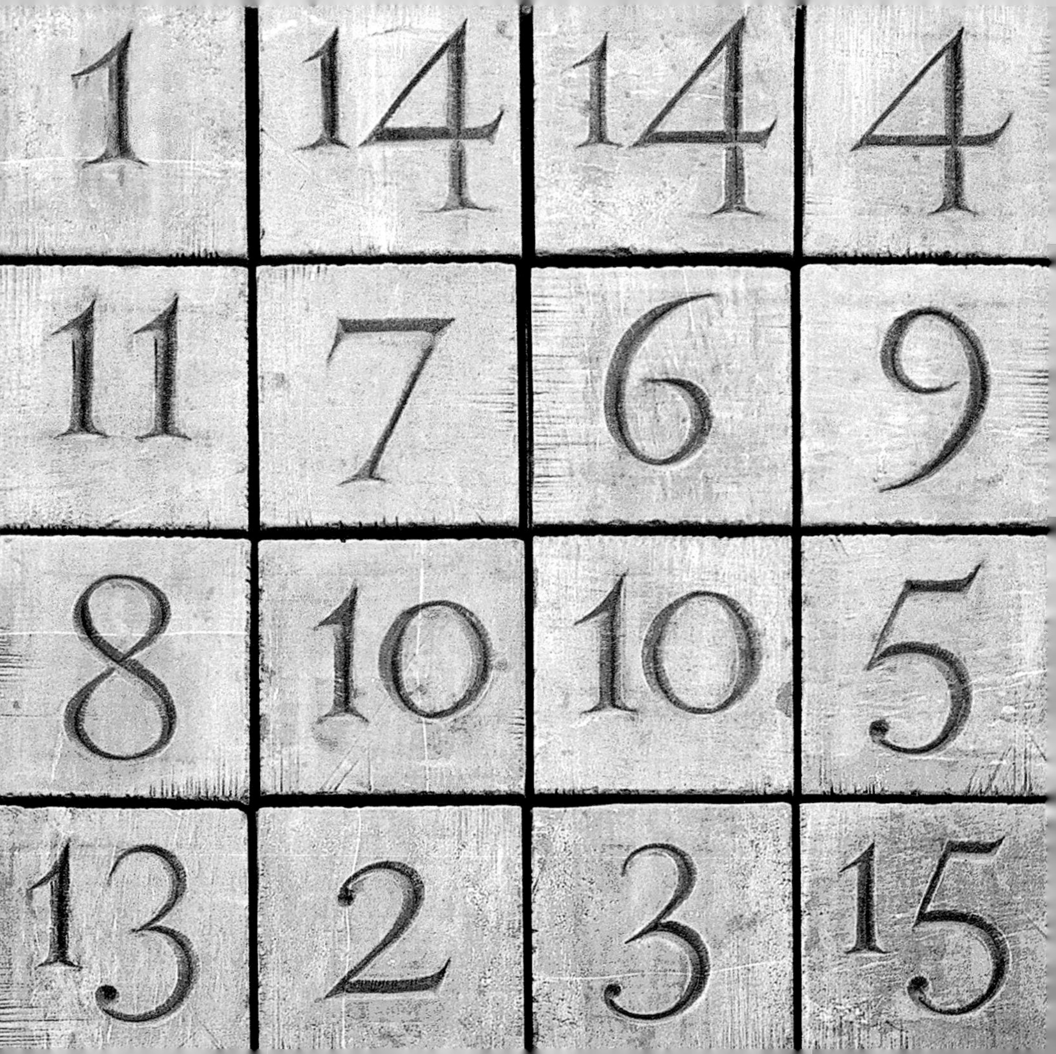
1 14 14 4
11 7 6 9
8 10 10 5
13 2 3 15

49

Betrayal of Judas

In the scene of the betrayal of Judas, who points out to the soldiers who Jesus Christ is with a kiss, human weakness and imperfection are synthesised, since Judas "marks" and gives away Jesus Christ with a kiss, and act of love and devotion.

As well as being an action of farewell or re-encounter, the kiss is an almost universal symbol of union, affection and adhesion. This is why it refers to the union and communion, and also to harmony, submission, respect and love.

In Christian liturgy, the veneration to the altar and the Gospel are expressed with a kiss. After reading the Gospel before the congregation, the book is kissed as a sign of faith and consideration for what it represents for the believing congregation. It is not, however, a kiss to the book as an object: in reality it is a kiss to Jesus Christ, who has spoken to the congregation through the book.

The fact that the action agreed by Judas and the soldiers who were going to arrest Jesus Christ was a kiss, the common greeting that began with the *shalom*, peace, becomes the betrayal of Judas in a doubly bloody and hateful act, since it perverts the deep symbolism of the kiss.

Behind Judas there is a snake, the animal that symbolises the lower world, matter and low passions. The snake has great symbolic richness, but in this case it symbolises the triumph of the material world, represented by bribery that according to tradition led Judas to deliver Jesus Christ to the "enemy". The stories of spies, double agents or denunciations come from long ago. The snake continues playing its role.

The figure of Judas is also a carrier of human imperfection, which means that the human world is imperfect by definition. In other words, perfection does not exist on the human plane. Even among the group of twelve apostles or disciples of Jesus Christ there is an element that does not fit, that breaks the harmony. Jesus Christ, given his divine condition, is perfectly aware that Judas was going to betray him, so if he had wanted to avoid it, he would have done so. This betrayal, however, formed part of the script of history, as a symbol of the imperfection of the human condition.

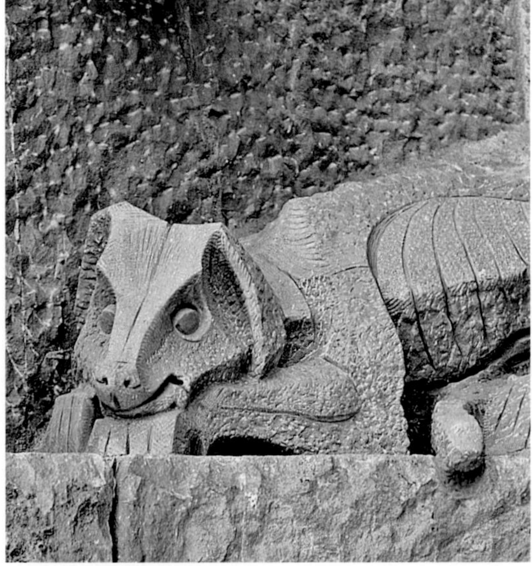

Sculptural series of the betrayal of Judas (right) and details: the kiss (above; the snake, which symbolises evil in the betrayal of Judas (centre) and the dog (below), which symbolises loyalty.

4
9
5
15

Flagellation

It occupies the lower central part, solitary, so that it has a great presence as part of the whole of the façade. To give it more dramatic effect, we would say that it is situated between the disciple who betrays him and the one who denies him three times.

The broken column symbolises the sinking of the old world with the coming of Jesus Christ. On a first level of interpretation the three steps symbolise the three days until the resurrection, but if we look for a deeper symbolism, we should consider that steps always symbolise the possibility of ascent or descent, of passing from one plane to another, of a gradual or stepped way, as the word itself indicates. In this case it is concerned with the possibility of spiritual ascent or salvation through the message of Jesus Christ. The knot, clearly visible, is the physical martyrdom, and the reed of the second square is the moral martyrdom.

From the point of view of established power, it is very logical that Jesus Christ is beaten, since the aim of flagellation is to symbolically and really destroy everything that may cause any type of disorder or disturbance at either a social or individual level. In past times and even today, flagellation is often a public spectacle, in order to emphasise its deterrent effect at a social level. With flagellation comes the re-establishing of the "normal" functioning of society. Of course Jesus Christ and the Christians in fact questioned the very social order of that Roman province. Therefore, the appropriate punishment for their leader was flagellation.

However, flagellation also has a shameful or derogatory nature, which makes it crueller. This is why it applied mainly to slaves, peasants, workers, soldiers and to rebellious children. The action of beating has as its aim to expel the demons from the body. It is probably this derogatory connotation that was taken into account when applying the punishment to Jesus Christ.

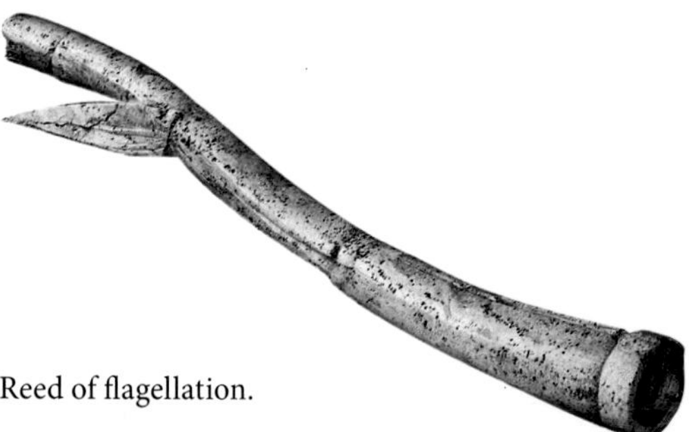

Reed of flagellation.

Alpha-Omega

Behind the image of Jesus Christ tied to the flagellation column, in the upper part of the mullion, there is an alpha and an omega, symbols of totality, which only God can achieve. If one considers that the alpha and the omega hold the key to the universe, what there is between alpha, the first letter of the Greek alphabet, and omega, the last letter, is, from a symbolic point of view, the universe in its totality.

The Apocalypse says: "and from Jesus Christ, who is the faithful witness, the first begotten of the dead, and the Prince of the Kings of the earth... I am Alpha and Omega, the beginning and the end, saith the Good Lord (the Father), who is, and who was, and who is to come, the Almighty". Therefore, God (Father and Son) is the beginning and end of all things. Later, also in the Apocalypse, it adds: "I am Alpha and Omega; the beginning and the end. To him that thirsteth, I will give of the fountain of the water of life, freely. He that shall overcome shall possess these things, and I will be his God; and he shall be my son." I do not think there is anything else to add.

The design by Josep Maria Subirachs of the alpha in positive or in relief and the omega in negative and one placed over the other has resulted in an interesting symmetrical figure. The arrangement of the alpha and the omega makes this rectangular figure express very graphically the idea of the totality of the cosmos. We could fold the image in half and the alpha would perfectly fit in the omega of the lower part.

Also, if we slide the alpha down and place the lower line in the middle of the omega, we would obtain the Star of David, also a symbol of totality. However, this figure is also the conjunction or cupola between the feminine and masculine triangles. The Star of David, as well as constituting the most emblematic symbol of the Hebrew tradition, is also a symbol of universal or cosmic polarity.

In this sense, the symbolism of the Star of David is almost equivalent to the symbolism of the cross and the symbolism of the Tai Chi (Yin-Yang), which also express totality from cosmic polarity. In the symbol of the Tai Chi the black point emerges from within the dynamic and white half circumference, and the white point emerges from the black half circumference, in order to graphically illustrate the unity that exists beneath the appearance of duality.

Jesus tied to the column of flagellation. Behind him, the symbol of totality: the alpha-omega.

Denials of Peter

Peter, the first apostle, also the first Bishop of Rome, the ancestor of the Holy Father, denies Jesus Christ. When he does it however, he does so more as an individual than as a representative of the apostles. We can say that he is the delegate of the disciples, and by extension all other humans, who denies him in his name. Not because Peter is particularly cowardly, but what Peter embodies with the three denials is the attitude, in some ways very human, of uncertainty and fear. Otherwise, the arrival of a prophet would not have been necessary, of an incarnation or of a Messiah. Peter acts, then, as a prototype of human beings.

In the setting, the three women embody the three times that Peter is questioned, and the cock recalls the cry of this animal after each denial. The cock is the solar animal par excellence and, therefore, symbol of renewal and resurrection, because the great "miracle" of the star-sun is that each day dies and a few hours later is resurrected. This is how man saw it in traditional societies.

The cock's cry announces the solar resurrection, and as the sun is the star associated with God, the cock is awake and ready to greet and receive the sun (Jesus Christ) even before it has risen in the east (the illumination). Therefore, when the cock crows after the denials of Peter, it is announcing that, despite the denial or condemnation, Jesus Christ, like the sun, will resuscitate or reappear. We can state that the denial of Peter represents the sunset, and the cock crowing, the dawn. Even more so when the master had already told the disciple that he would deny him three times before dawn.

Just like if there were no darkness there would be no light or if the sun did not set then obviously it would not rise, if Peter had not denied Christ, the cock would not have responded confirming his resurrection. This operation is repeated three times, because this number is, among many other things, the number of the basic cycle and, in this sense, it is the number of self-sufficiency, because three is the internal development of unity or beginning of everything.

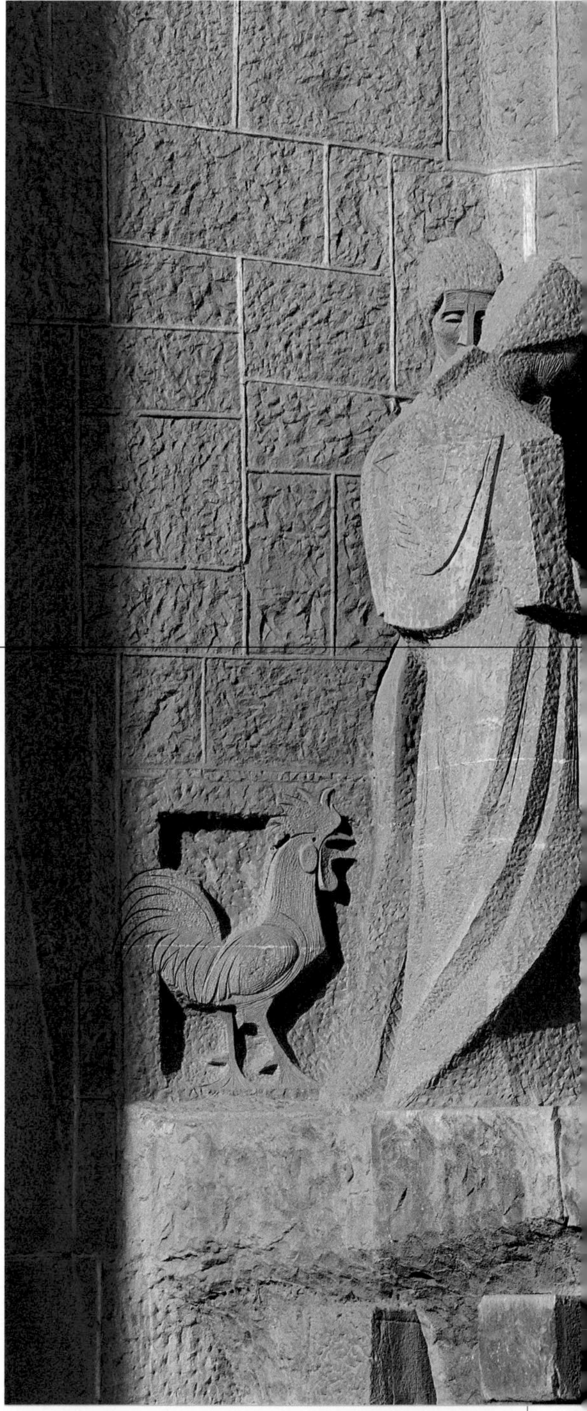

Detail of the cock that crowed after the three denials of Peter.

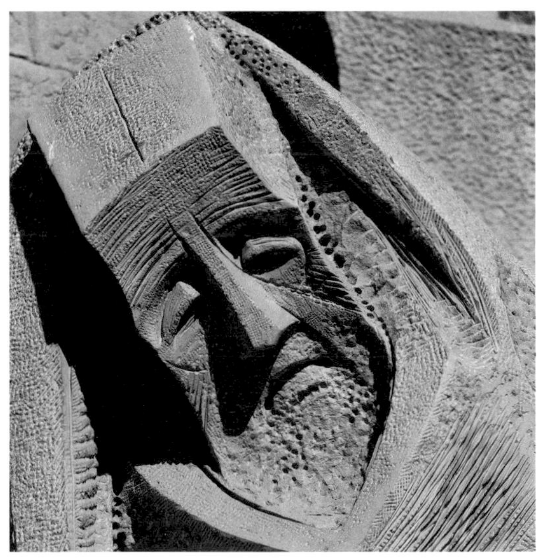

Shameful face of Peter after denying knowledge of the master three times.

Face of one of the three women that symbolise the three times that Peter denied Jesus Christ.

Labyrinth

Between the series of the denial of Peter and the house of the high priest there is a labyrinth, which, in the first instance is the route of the passion of Jesus Christ, the painful itinerary that begins at that moment.

To start with, a labyrinth is a way of protecting the centre, which is what allows access to sacrality. It is the point where the transformation of the Self occurs, since it is the point of arrival of the journey which goes from the darkness to the light. It is also the point where the spirit triumphs over matter and the eternal over the mortal, intelligence over instinct, in brief, the liberating message of Jesus Christ. The symbolism of this labyrinth is closely linked to the labyrinths that make up the symbolism of the cross, since we find ourselves before the façade in which Jesus Christ dies on the cross. The symbolism of these labyrinths in the form of a cross is "the divine inscrutability". For mortals, wanting to know the divine will is more difficult that penetrating a complex labyrinth.

No mortal is capable of understanding the dimension of which the passion and death of Jesus Christ began. The reasons for the divine will are impossible to understand for human beings. It is that of the curved lines or of which the paths of the Lord are inscrutable.

In a cathedral, the labyrinth has another meaning: going through the labyrinth is equivalent to going on a pilgrimage to the Holy Land. Those who, for whatever circumstance, do not have the possibility of going to Jerusalem, can follow the route of the labyrinth, since reaching its centre is like reaching the city of Jerusalem, the symbolic centre of the Christian world.

For many riverside cultures of the Mediterranean, a labyrinth placed on the door or façade of a house is an element of protection. Its function is similar to that of the representation of monsters whose mission is to frighten the enemy. The labyrinth of the door impedes the entry of enemies, since it was believed that hostile and negative forces could only advance in straight lines and would get lost in the labyrinth. In this case the labyrinth can also be an element of protection of the temple.

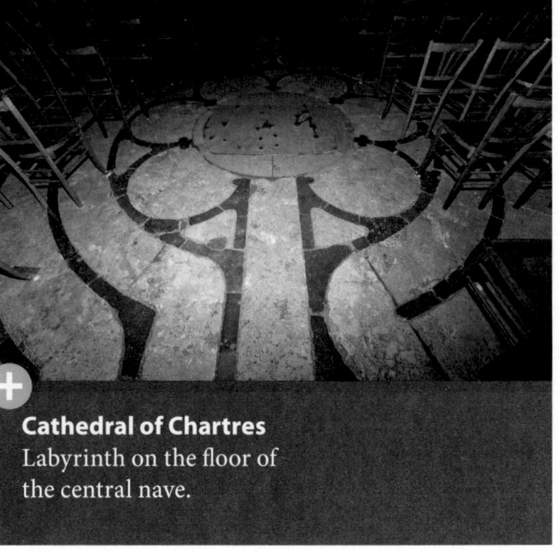

Cathedral of Chartres
Labyrinth on the floor of the central nave.

Like medieval labyrinths, this one is also the symbol of inscrutability.

Crown of thorns

A crown is clearly a solar symbol and due to its roundness is also a symbol of totality and perfection. However, the crown of thorns that they place on Jesus Christ as an element of torture, and also of ridicule, has a very deep symbolism that transcends these mean acts and human injustices.

The crown is an element of participation in heavenly nature; whoever wears it is joined to all there is below him and all there is above him. As a result, it is a promise of the immortal life of the gods. The crown of Jesus Christ symbolises, therefore, the immortality of his message.

The symbolism of the crown ends taking shape according to the material with which it is made. A crown of gold is clearly a solar symbol of power and centrality, obviously highly appropriate for kings.

If thorns symbolise the virgin or unploughed land, the crown of thorns —replaced at weddings by the crown of orange blossom flowers— represent the virginity of woman and the earth. The crown of thorns of the passion of Jesus Christ celebrates the marriage between heaven or the divine influence and the virgin land or terrestrial earth. It is like the marriage ring or alliance between the message of Jesus Christ and the virgin earth that must be fertilised or saved.

According to the legend, the crown of Jesus Christ was made of acacia thorns. The acacia is the tree that symbolises the resurrection and immortality. In this same sense, it represents the eternal line of what is called perennial religion which through historic contingencies is a carrier of wisdom and knowledge.

The crown of thorns of Jesus Christ is thus a twofold symbol of immortality, both for the object in itself and for the material of which it is made: the immortality of the marriage between the divine influence and the land or the fertilising action of the spiritual world in the material world. The crown of thorns is the symbol of the immortality of the message of Jesus Christ.

Jesus before Pontius Pilate

The last group on the right of the first level of the façade is broken down into two moments: in the first, Pontius Pilate presents Jesus as *Ecce Homo*, and in the second, Pontius Pilate washes his hands.

Although washing one's hands is a practically universal symbol of inner purity, in this case it does not have this meaning. Given that the hands are the symbol of rational action of human beings in the reality that surrounds them, washing them signifies the purity and integrity of the works they undertake with these clean hands. In the case of Pontius Pilate, what this represents is that he does not share the desire of the high priests, that he does not want to be co-responsible for the crucifixion of Jesus Christ. In reality, however, what he is doing is purifying before even having his hands stained with blood. He adopts a preventive measure for the consequences that that dubious trial might have. He washes his hands before getting them dirty.

The action of washing one's hands is also the gesture of ritual purification prior to all sacrifices. The passion and death of Jesus Christ is clearly a sacrifice; a very special sacrifice, in which God offers his own son, and also a sacrifice for the salvation of all humanity. Pontius Pilate thus participates in the universal liturgy of all sacrifices.

The silence of Jesus Christ before Pontius Pilate is not arrogance or lack of argument; it is simply that he does not fear death, or the transformation that death involves. Moreover, in his case it is the reason he has been made man and for which he is the bearer of the message of salvation for humanity. Therefore, it would make no sense whatsoever to struggle to change the course of events as they unfold.

Sculptural group of Jesus before Pontius Pilate and details: the hands of Jesus and Pontius Pilate washing his hands.

56

Way of the Calvary

On the second level are represented the scenes of the climb to the Calvary. In the first group on the right is Jesus fallen, Simon of Cyrene, the Cyrenian who helped him carry the cross. We also see the Virgin, with her sister and aunt of Jesus Christ, Mary of Cleophas and Mary Magdalene, watching horrified.

According to some versions. The soldiers who were watching over Jesus Christ did not wait for him to fall before ordering the Cyrenian to help him carry the cross. He would, from the start have carried it at the orders of the soldiers. Therefore, walking in a dignified way, Jesus Christ would have preceded the Cyrenian, who would carry the cross on his neck. This version takes away much drama from the way of the Calvary.

According to this same version, Jesus Christ would have reached the foot of the cross in a perfect state and the soldiers themselves had offered him a sedative drink that would enable him to withstand the pain of the crucifixion, wine and myrrh. However, Jesus Christ would have refused it. Clearly, he did not want to experience a moment as transcendental as death at the cross under the effects of a sedative. It would have been totally inconceivable and illogical. Moreover, for the son of God the experience of pain and suffering is not the same as any other mortal experiences.

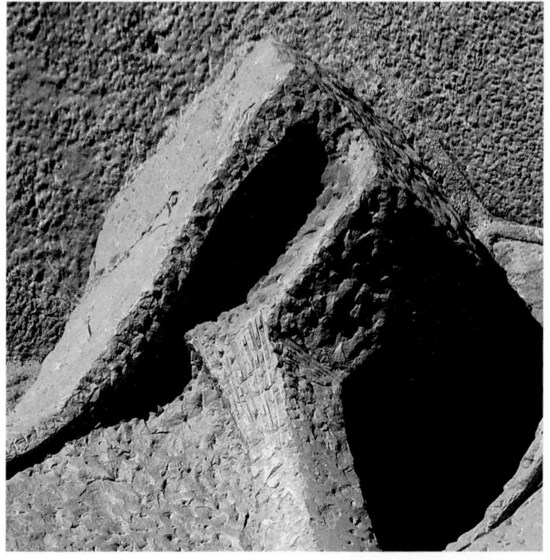

Covered face of one of the three Marys.

Simon of Cyrene helping Jesus carry the cross, while Mary, her sister and Mary Magdalene cover their faces horrified.

Veronica

In this series the second fall and the meeting with the women from Jerusalem is represented, among whom the symbolic figure of the Veronica is featured, who shows the effigy of Jesus, which, through an optical effect, seems to be always turning towards the spectator.

This optical effect underlines the importance of the eyes in daily life, since they constitute a first-class element of communication. The fact of looking towards a place or a person is of great relevance. With a look one can express many things. The fact of looking or not at the interlocutor in the eyes also says a lot. In fact, through the eyes of a look one can express or "say" many things. With the look one speaks. When we say that the eyes are a reflection of the soul, we are referring to this. In reality it is one of the first elements of communication; even before communicating with each other through speaking, we communicate through our eyes, and with a look we know if we are welcome or not.

The eyes of Jesus Christ are the look of God. It seems that the look of Jesus Christ was one of the things that most impressed his disciples. The Gospels often mention this. It was not an aggressive look but a very observant one, which let no detail fall by the way. Strictly speaking, we can say that he saw everything. Therefore, in this series of the Passion Façade the look of the effigy of Jesus Christ in the sheet of the Veronica is the look of God. Because he sees all. Wherever you stand, he is looking at you. It is the belief that God sees all.

The most outstanding element of the pair of soldiers are the helmets, a clear homage by Subirachs to Gaudí, since they vividly recall the chimneys of the Casa Milà (La Pedrera), of which it has always been said were the helmets of medieval knights. Further to the left of this group we come across the figure of an evangelist that is noting down what is happening, in other words, a chronicler of history. This evangelist emphasises the homage by Subirachs to Gaudí, since the face of the figure is the portrait of the brilliant architect.

The face of Jesus Christ marked on the robe of Veronica, who, through an optical effect, is always looking at the observer.

Detail of the faceless Veronica highlights the face of Jesus Christ (above and right) and the sculptural series of the second fall of Jesus (following).

The face of the evangelist situated to the left of the sculptural group and who is recording what is happening, clearly reproduces the face of Gaudí in the photograph published of the Procession of Corpus Christi in Barcelona.

La Pedrera (Casa Milà)
Crowning of the chimney of La Pedrera inspired by the helmets of the Roman soldiers.

Longinus

He is the centurion who, with his spear, injured Jesus Christ on his right side and who later converted to Christianity. In the sculpture he is on horseback and the spear crosses the façade. From this wound on the side flowed blood and water. This action symbolises the birth of the Christian Church, since water and blood represent the basic sacraments: baptism and the Eucharist.

Curiously, Longinus was a fellow countryman of Antoni Gaudí, since it is believed that the Roman soldier was from *Tarraconense*. It was the custom for governors from the provinces to have a personal guard of the utmost trust and loyalty who accompanied them wherever they went. This guard was formed in the first destination of that the governor had command of. Pontius Pilate's first destination was *Tarraconense*, so that his personal guard was made up of soldiers who came from this province. And the governor's personal guard —remember that it was considered of the utmost trust— was in charge of controlling the delicate mission of keeping watch on that dangerous character called Jesus Christ who died crucified. Thus, Longinus and the other members of Pontius Pilate's personal guard presumably came from *Tarraconense*.

The spear that crosses the façade is the spear that crossed the right side of Jesus Christ, agonizing on the cross. In this sense, the Temple of the Sagrada Família assimilates the body of Jesus Christ, drawing a clear parallel between the house of God and the body of God. Remember that every church should be considered from a threefold point of view: as the body of Jesus Christ, as a church and as the union of the souls of the believers.

In contrast with the sword, which is a heavenly weapon, the spear is considered an earthly weapon. In general, the symbolism of the spear is also related to that of the tree and the cross, symbols of the valley-mountain axis. The symbolism of the spear is also related to that of the glass, and in this case to the glass that collects the blood of Jesus Christ, in other words, the Grail, the Holy Grail or, for some, royal blood.

If making a judgement about intentions is always risky, in this case it is even more so. Nevertheless, it appears that Longinus's intention was not to finish off Jesus Christ but to extract his blood, with all the symbolism that this vital flow has and which we have already seen in the series of the Last Supper.

59

Playing for the robes

In the first group on the third level on the left, the soldiers play for Jesus' robes. The table they are playing on is a massive astragal, the lamb bone that preceded the dice of today.

The Romans were so fond of dice games that for a time they had to prohibit them. The ban was only lifted during the festivals of Saturnalia. It is said that the emperors Augustus, Nero and Claudius were hardened players, what today we would call compulsive gamblers. It was also a game that was very popular amongst the militias of that time. It is therefore historically correct for the Roman soldiers to gamble for the robes by throwing the dice.

Symbolically a dice represents the perfection and solidity of matter, since the cube-shaped dice, on being the square of a square, is the volume of matter. However, if you unfold a cube on a flat surface and it goes from being a three-dimensional figure to a two-dimensional one, we find ourselves before a Latin cross; the cross on which Jesus Christ died crucified and which is the central motif of this façade.

The robes or objects that belonged or belong to someone are carriers of the energy of that person. This is the justification of reliquaries.
In consequence, we can say that the robes of Jesus Christ were impregnated with his energy or his message, and that the soldiers that shared them out were sharing out the inheritance or message of Jesus Christ through his clothing.

In the sharing out of this inheritance, the introduction of the random factor of playing dice indicates the universality of Jesus Christ, and that his message is for the whole world, since chance unites us to everyone. Another question is whether chance exists and that when we say something happens by chance we are showing our ignorance about the reason why. Said another way, there are no coincidences and everything is coincidence. What happens is that we do not know their cause-effect relationship.

The fact that the soldiers chose to play dice for the robes instead of dividing them into the corresponding parts and each one getting their share, it symbolises the indivisibility of the message of Jesus Christ. There are things that cannot be divided, that cannot be compartmentalised. They form a unit, a whole, and that is how they should be treated.

Jackstones (a very popular game among the Romans) from the Museum of the History of Barcelona. The jack is the bone known as astragalus, the shape of which inspired the table over which the soldiers are playing for the robes of Jesus.

Crucifixion

The central and culminating scene of this façade is that of Jesus on the cross. On the right of the crucified are the *Virgin* Mary, Mary Magdalene and Saint John; to the left, the skull of Adam, the entrance to the sepulchre with the stone and the moon. The presence of a skull refers to the name of Golgotha, which means "mountain of the skull", but also refers to the skull of Adam, the skull of the first man.

In the symbolism of the cross we find two aspects: that of the cross in itself and that of the crucifixion, that is, "being on the cross". The Latin cross on which Jesus Christ dies crucified represents the conjunction of the two opposites, of the cosmic duality: the positive is the vertical post and the negative the horizontal crosspiece. This cosmic duality has other realisations, black-white, male-female, up-down, etc., but in the Latin cross the negative crosspiece is raised by the positive vertical post. In the dialectic between the two poles, the positive rises and overcomes the negative.

The crucifixion is the essential experience of antagonism created by existence, the uncertainty and agony the cross creates from possibility and impossibility, from essence and power, from construction and deconstruction. Numerologically, we can say that the 2 (vertical line and horizontal line) becomes 4 (material world —water, earth, air and fire—) through 3 (the conjunction of the cosmic duality plus Jesus Christ, or the Holy Trinity, or brimstone —vertical—, salt —horizontal— and mercury —centre of the cross—). Number 2 also comes from 1, because it is God, unity, which makes man, who passes to the manifest world, the dual world, to the 2.

The six-armed cross, that of the crucifixion of Jesus Christ on this façade and which Gaudí liked so much, present in other buildings such as Casa Milà or Park Güell, strengthens the idea of the step from 2 to 4, or what amounts to the same thing, from the manifest to the material.

The duality of the cross is strengthened by the presence of pairs of opposites, particularly present in medieval iconography. We thus encounter the cross between the sun and the moon, between the Virgin Mary and Saint John, between the good thief and the bad thief, between heaven and earth, etc. In this sculptural series, Subirachs has pointed to this medieval tendency, but only as an insinuation: on one side the moon, on the other, the Virgin, the favourite disciple and Mary Magdalene. They are incomplete cosmic dualities that recall the authentic dualities of medieval iconography, and which become references for those who are scholars.

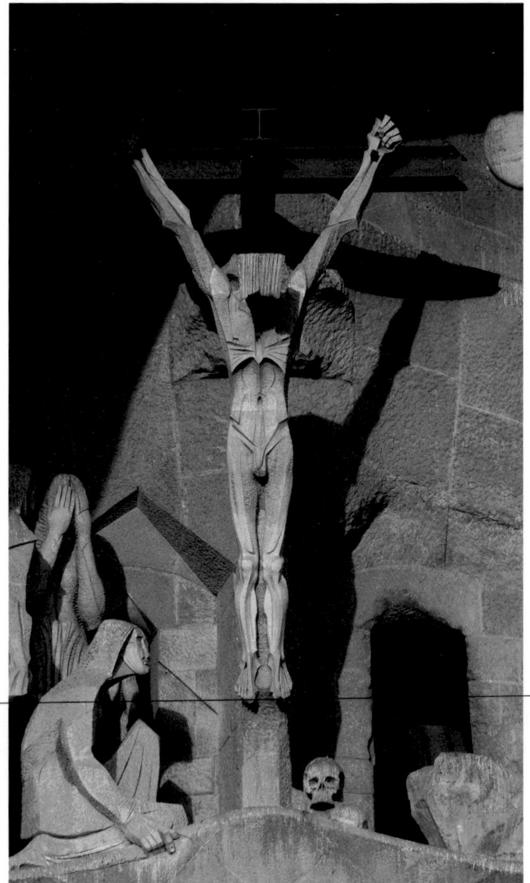

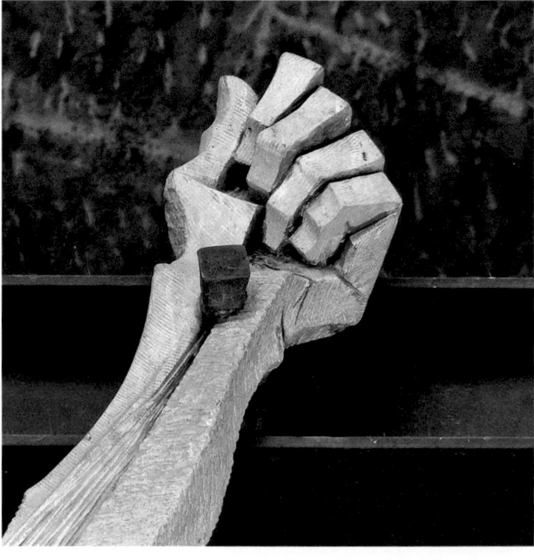

The cross is, generally, a symbol of meeting or crossing between two realities. In this sense, it is also the symbol of synthesis, since thesis and antithesis are surpassed by synthesis. And in the crucifixion, synthesis is the son of God who dies on the cross to save humanity.

The outline of the beams that form the cross has the form of an "I", the first letter of the sign INRI, which Pontius Pilate had put on the cross.

61

Sepulchre

The sepulchre is where symbolically the purification of God made man, Jesus Christ, takes place. Like the cave, it is the crucible where during the three symbolic days the alchemical transmutation occurs. It is, strictly speaking, where the return journey takes place. The outward journey occurs when the son of God is made man; he now abandons this temporary situation, because his mission has ended, his work is done. Jesus Christ abandoned the human condition and returned to his original and eternal condition, the divine condition.

As has already been hinted at, the sepulchre or tomb is equivalent to the symbols of gestation, generation or fertility, such as the egg. In a large number of prehistoric sepulchres, discovered in what are today Russia and Sweden, we can find clay eggs that symbolise immortality. The eggs that are our Easter eggs clearly refer to this symbolism of regeneration, in other words, death and resurrection. The egg is, as a way of saying, both sepulchre and nest at the same time. It is so in the meaning of profound transformation, in that for something to be born, another thing must die. For a tree to be born, its seed must die; or the caterpillar must die for the butterfly to be born; or the sea water must die to become clouds and later rainwater. In reality, it is about the death and birth of the external aspect and of the permanence of what is substantial.

It is in privileged and special places, closed, isolated and protected from the outside world where the processes of transmutation take place. These spaces must comply with a series of conditions, such as those of the fertile earth that must make the growth of the seed possible.

The death of God made man and the "resurrection" in divine God is also the model for many initiation ceremonies, in which the precious being dies symbolically and the new human being is born as a result of the initiation. This model or initiation ceremony is not original to Jesus Christ, but is a practically universal model, before or after Jesus Christ. What is original and innovative is that it is about a possibility of change or birth of a new world that is made accessible to all; it is a message for the whole community.

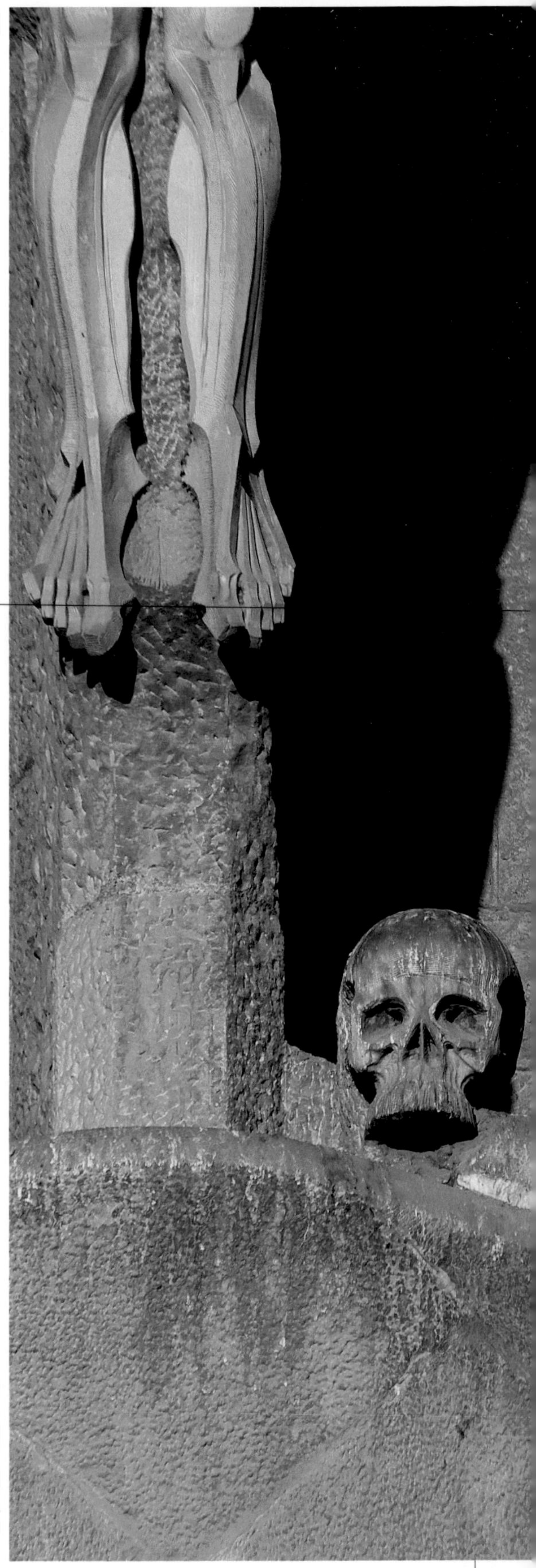

The skull at the foot of the cross evokes the name of Mount Golgotha. The open sepulchre indicates the resurrection of Jesus.

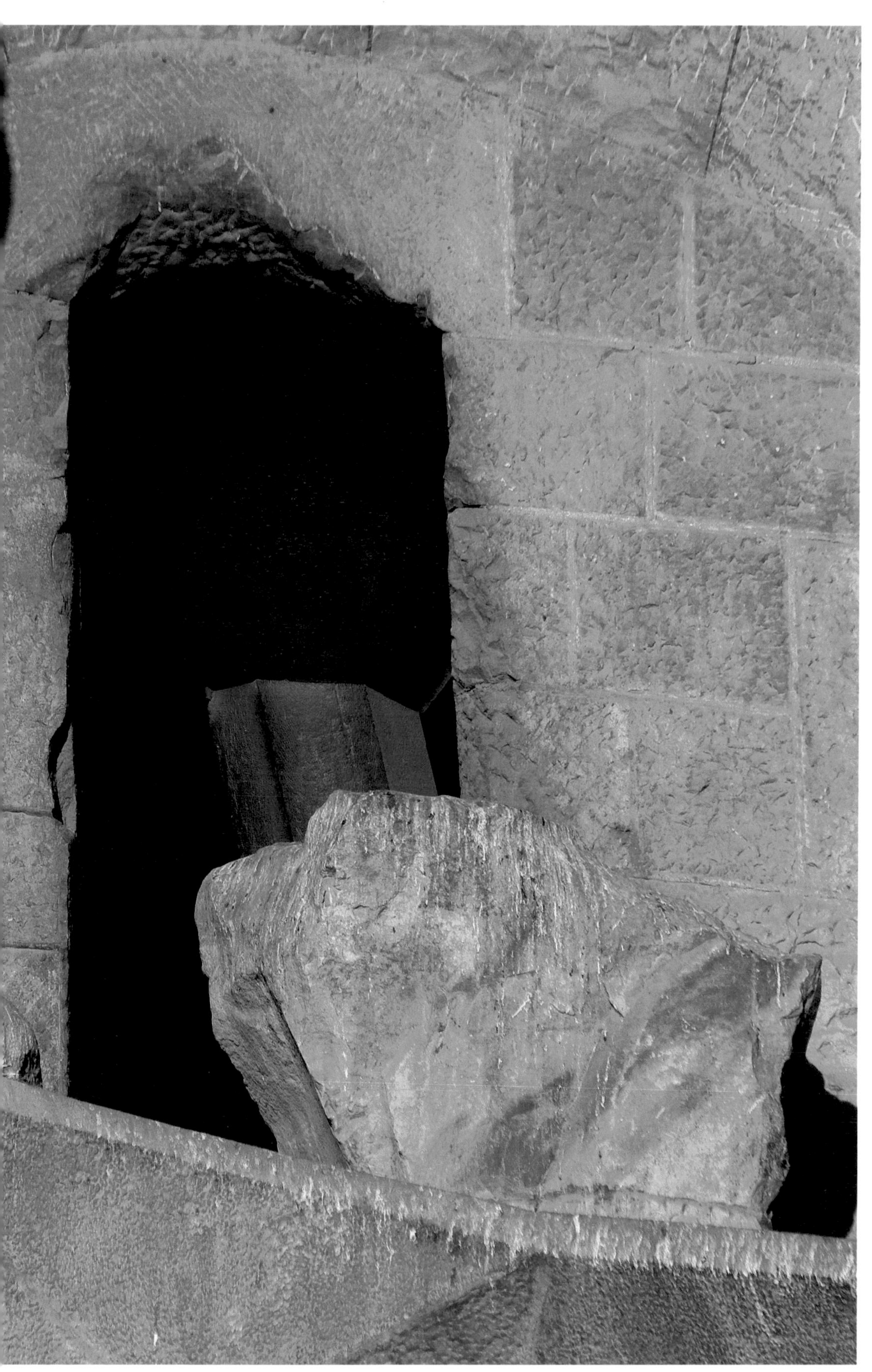

The burial

The last group represents the burial. In the foreground, Joseph of Arimathea and Nicodemus place the shrouded body in the tomb. Behind them is the Virgin Mary, and in the background, over the door of the sepulchre, a large egg, which in this case symbolises the resurrection (we find this same symbol in the Virgin by Piero della Francesca and in the *Madonna of Portlligat* by Salvador Dalí).

Burial, following the ritual of every religion or tradition, is the first and essential step for achieving eternal life, salvation, or whatever we want to call it; this shows the importance and respect that it is usually afforded. Nevertheless, in this case the mortal to be buried was very special: it was God made man. As a human being he had to take part in the burial ritual, but as divinity he was at the margin of this contingency, and on the third day —3 is the spiritual number in as much as it surpasses 2, number of the manifest— he arose and, as one way of saying it, left behind his human appearance. One can say that the mission of Jesus Christ had ended.

The idea of the resurrection is perfectly expressed in the egg, which is no other than the Easter egg, when Jesus Christ rises from the dead. The Easter egg is the egg of periodical and cyclical renewal but it is also the egg of resurrection, which is also a form of renewal. One of the most followed traditions of the Oriental Orthodox Church is that of Easter. When at the banquet each diner fervently toasts their red painted egg with their neighbour and says, "Christ is resurrected", the egg that breaks is the sepulchre that opens and allows the resurrection of Jesus Christ; it is the egg that becomes the seed of new life, life after death, eternal life; it is at the same time the tomb and seed of life, it is the symbol of the Trinity revealed. On this same line, it is logical that it is identified with the resurrection of nature, since it is at Easter or in spring when nature abandons the tomb of winter. The Easter egg is both tomb and nest, because without a prior death, represented by the symbolism of the tomb, there can be no birth or rebirth, represented by the nest. The egg placed above the entrance of the sepulchre announces or prefigures this double symbolism.

Detail of Nicodemus (very similar to the sculptor J. M. Subirachs) depositing the body of Jesus Christ in the sepulchre.

Brera Art Gallery. Milan
Piero della Francesca already used the egg as a symbol of the resurrection of Jesus Christ in the *Virgin Mary* of the Brera Art Gallery (fragment).

Glory, Heaven or Life Façade

"The fragment of the model of the bell towers of the main façade will not be completed or developed. I have decided to leave it only programmed for another generation to work on the temple, as has been seen repeatedly in the history of cathedrals, the façades of which are not only by other authors, but also of other styles."

Antoni Gaudí

Of the grand façade that forms the main entrance to the temple, Gaudí left us only the structural study and the iconographic and symbolic plan. As corresponds to the main façade of a temple, it will comment on the life and destiny of man, heaven or hell, depending on whether their life is worthy of reward or punishment. Isidre Puig i Boada, disciple, collaborator and scholar of Gaudí, wrote: "The Glory Doorway, unfinished symphony, magnificent and total orchestration of the Dogma and of the complete problem of the life of man".

It will represent man before sin and how, after the original sin, he was condemned to work. On the main façade, on a porch, the life of work of man with the many trades: tailor, cobbler and others. It will show the human being within the general order of creation, explaining to him what is his origin, which makes sense of his existence and which paths he should follow.

Through work and with the practice of virtue, the human being can reach Glory, assisted by the fruit of redemption and for the grace of the Holy Spirit. The realisation is a very clear Manichean approach. The final consequence of sin is hell and the consequence of virtue is heaven. Moreover, spiritual life is nourished by prayer and the sacraments.

On this façade, distributed hierarchically in the form of a pyramid, the following elements will appear symbolised, in ascending order: hell, death, the vices, the virtues, the gifts of the Holy Spirit, the sacraments, the Lord's Prayer, the acts of mercy, Adam and Eve, Saint Joseph, the manual trades, the Beatitudes, the Virgin and the saints, Jesus

Photograph of the original model by Gaudí of the Glory Façade (below) and drawing of it (right) by Francesc Berenguer.

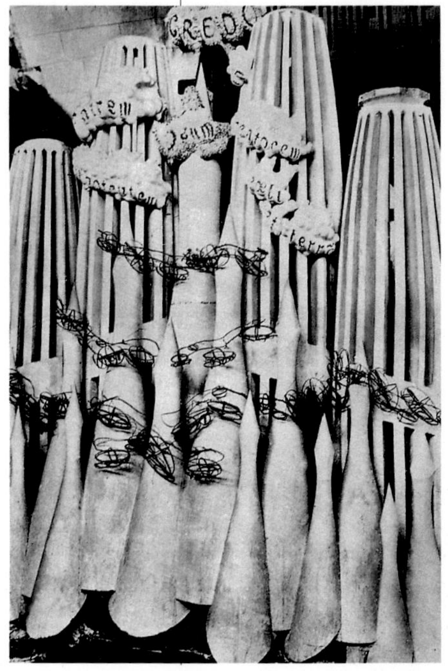

CREDO
unum
Patrem
omnipotentem
Deum factorem
cœli
et terræ
Ecclesiam
Amen
amen
Pax

Christ the judge, the creation, the Creed, faith, hope and charity, the angelic hierarchies and, at the very top, the august Trinity. The Glory Façade will be like a massive pantocrator.

It will go in crescendo, from Hell to Heaven. On the lowest plane, logically, will be placed Hell, on the vaults and pillars of the tunnel that support the platform and entrance stairway to the temple. Here we will find all of the demonic "pagan" and mythological representations, the heresies, the schisms, the apostasies, etc., all the elements of the "outer shadows". Along the edges of the chandeliers that will be like a moat and which will provide light in the tunnel, some of these hellish creatures will stick out their heads in order to witness the triumph of Jesus Christ and of the Church, which is the imposing façade of the Glory Façade.

This moat where Hell is situated is the *mundus* that the Romans dug when they built a city. It is the world of the subterranean and infernal regions. The *mundus* was the place where one entered into contact with all this sub-world. This moat, which is like the gateway to Hell, allowed offerings and sacrifices to be made to the forces and gods of this sub-world. The hole was then covered and made into a buttress of the city that would also serve as protection from diabolical forces.

The *mundus* or Hell is a way of taming the forces of evil. The reasoning is the following: since they are there, we do not ignore them, making them present and giving them their own space while removing strength and power from them. We recognise and accept their presence and we take away a large part of their importance. In current terms, we can say that there is a possibility for dialogue. This function is what current psychoanalytical currents think about, when they say that there must be conflicts or shadows of our personality, never concealing them, because it is the best way of controlling them and removing their importance.

In the Sagrada Família the moat of the Glory Façade will serve as the *mundus*, the place where Hell is situated. It should be stated that nearly all cathedrals have their *mundus*, their own infernal territory; it was the place

Section of the Temple where one can appreciate the tunnel through which Carrer Mallorca will run before the Glory Façade.

(Right page) Symbolic programme of the Glory Façade.

Sanctus
Sanctus
Sanctus
Sanctus

Sanctus
Sanctus
Sanctus
Sanctus
Sanctus
Sanctus

Making a dream come true

This comparative chronology covers the time from when the temple's promoter, Josep Maria Bocabella, had a dream about building the temple (1877), until Gaudí's death (1926). It also includes the political and cultural events relevant to the history of Catalonia and Spain (some of particular importance in the life of Gaudí), as well as showing what was developed in the field of science and art and which represented a landmark in the history of western culture.

"The work of the Sagrada Família is slow because the owner of this work is in no hurry".
Antoni Gaudí

Josep Maria Bocabella bought the site where the Temple would be built for 172,000 pesetas.

Comparative chronology 1877-1926

H HISTORY
G GAUDÍ
A ARTS
S SCIENCE AND TECHNOLOGY
R RELIGION

1877
A Verdaguer publishes *L'Atlàntida.*
A Tolstoy publishes *Anna Karenina.*
A Dostoyevsky publishes *The Dream of a Ridiculous Man.*
A Monet paints *Interior of the Saint-Lazare Station.*

1878
G Gaudí designs the lampposts in the Plaça Reial in Barcelona.

1879
A Lluís Domènech i Montaner constructs the building of the Montaner y Simón publishing house.
S Thomas Edison develops the first electric light bulb.

1880
A Rodin sculpts *The Thinker.*
A Maupassant publishes *Soirées de Medan*, considered the Naturalist Manifesto.

1881
A Monet paints *Snowy landscape at dusk.*
A Richard Wagner premieres *Parsifal.*
R Proclamation of the Virgin of Montserrat as patron saint of Catalonia.

1882
A William Le Baron Jenney builds the first skyscraper in Chicago.
A Manet paints *The bar of the Folies Bergère*

1883
G Antoni Gaudí begins El Capricho and Casa Vicens.
A John Augusto Roebling completes Brooklyn Bridge.

1884
A The angular stone of the Statue of liberty is laid.
A Leopoldo Alas "Clarín" publishes *La Regenta.*

1882

1885

H King Alfonso XII of Spain dies. The reign of María Cristina begins.

A Nietzsche publishes *Zarathustra.*

A Verdaguer publishes *Canigó.*

S Louis Pasteur develops the anti-rabies vaccine.

1886

H Valentí Almirall publishes *Lo Catalanisme,* the first work that lays out the principles of political doctrine of Catalan autonomy.

A Jean Moréas publishes the Symbolist Manifest in Le Figaró.

G Gaudí builds the Palau Güell and the iron gateway of the dragon in Pedralbes.

S Karl Benz patents the first automobile.

1887

A Renoir paints *The Large Bathers.*

1888

H The UGT is founded in Barcelona (General Union of Workers)

H The Universal Exhibition of Barcelona is held.

A Josep Vilaseca builds the Arc de Triomf of Barcelona.

A Gaietà Buigas builds the Monument to Columbus in Barcelona.

The first stone of the Sagrada Família is laid under the direction of Francesc de Paula del Villar.

1882

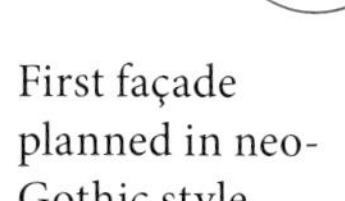

First façade planned in neo-Gothic style.

On the 3 November the young architect Gaudí takes over the direction of the Sagrada Família.

1883

C

1886

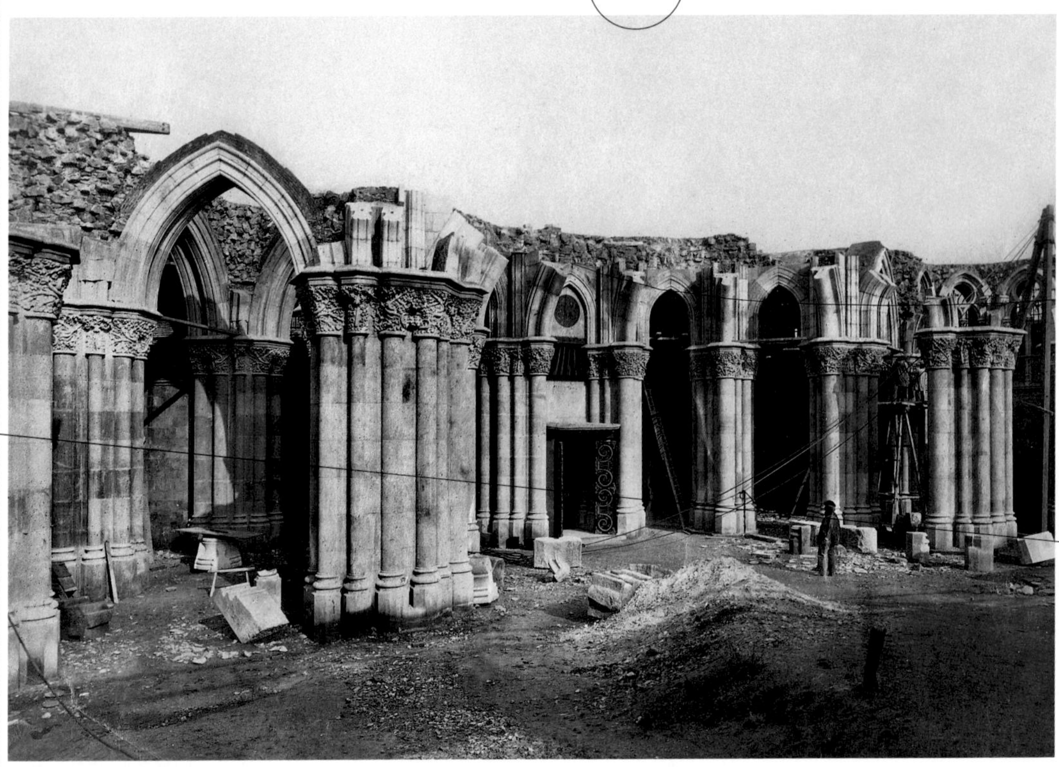

One of the first photographs of the works of the crypt.

The lower part of the apse maintains the neo-Gothic style of the crypt.

1889

H The Second International is founded.

G Gaudí completes the works on the Theresan College.

A Gustave Eiffel opens the Eiffel Tower in Paris.

A Louis Sullivan and Dankmar Adler complete the Auditorium in Chicago.

A Gauguin paints *The Yellow Christ*.

A Van Gogh paints *Wheatfield*.

1890

A Art Nouveau develops in Belgium.

A Emile Zola publishes *La Bête Humaine*.

1891

A The Orfeó Català is founded.

A Oscar Wilde publishes *The portrait of Dorian Gray*.

R Declaration of Saint Joseph (19 March) as an official holiday in Spain.

R Pope Leo XIII announces the encyclical letter *Rerum Novarum* about the situation of the workers.

1892

H *Bases de Manresa*, the Unió Catalanista produces the document for the Catalan regional constitution.

1893

H Anarchist bomb in the Liceu.

A Victor Horta builds the Tassel House in Brussels.

A Foundation of the Cercle Artístic Sant Lluc.

A Restoration of the monastery of Ripoll.

A Munch paints *The Scream*.

S Henry Ford builds his first car.

1894

G Exhausting Lent fast by Gaudí places his life in danger.

A Debussy premieres *Prélude à l'après-midi d'un faune*.

1895

H The Spanish-American War begins.

First steps in the construction of the Nativity Façade.

1896

1903

N.º 177. BARCELONA
TEMPLO DE LA SAGRADA FAMILIA

N.º 115. BARCELONA
TEMPLO DE LA SAGRADA FAMILIA

1906

First postcards of the works of the Temple.

A. T. V. — 47 - BARCELON
Iglesia de la Sagrada Familia
Fachada princi

1906

C

The surroundings of the temple still preserve wasteland where the herds of goats graze.

1905

In this year, Joan Maragall publishes "A favour of charity" about the Sagrada Família.

1905

A Francesc Berenguer builds the Bodegas Güell in Garraf.
S The Lumière brothers present the first cinematographic projection.
S Röntgen discovers X-rays.

1896
A Joseph Maria Olbrich completes the Secession Building in Vienna.
A Anton Chekhov publishes *The Seagull.*
S Marconi patents the radio.

1897
A Charles Rennie Mackintosh begins construction work on the Glasgow School of Art.
A Stoker writes *Dracula.*

1898
H Loss of the last Spanish colonies.

G Gaudí builds the Casa Calvet.
A The Saint Paul's building in New York is completed, one of the tallest in the world.
A Works begin on the Casa Amatller by Josep Puig i Cadafalch.

1899
H FC Barcelona is founded.
A Monet paints *Japanese Bridge.*

1900
G Antoni Gaudí begins work on Park Güell.
A Hector Guimard designs the entrances to the stations of the Paris metro.
A Puccini premieres *Tosca* in Rome.
A John Ruskin dies.
S Ferdinand von Zeppelin makes the Zeppelin fly for the first time.

1901
A Josep Puig i Cadafalch builds the Palau Macaya.
A Domènech i Montaner produces the project for the Hospital de Sant Pau.
A Klimt paints *Judith I*

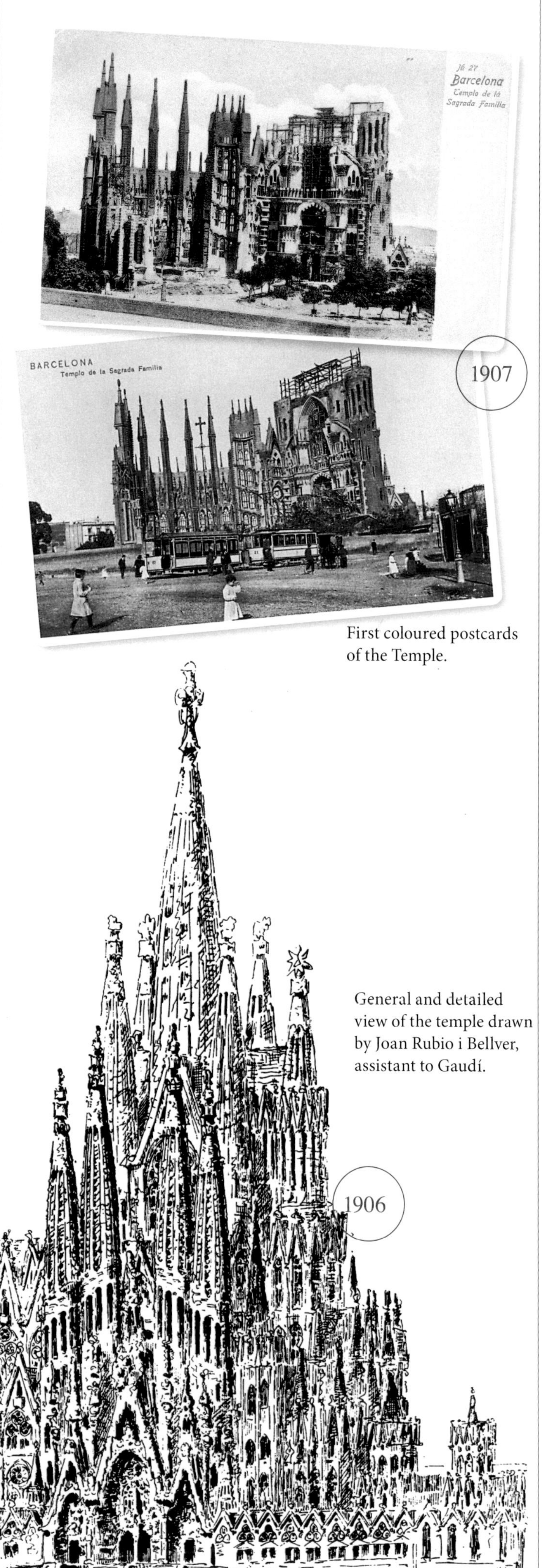

1907

First coloured postcards of the Temple.

1906

General and detailed view of the temple drawn by Joan Rubio i Bellver, assistant to Gaudí.

1908

Model of the Nativity Façade, decorated by J. M. Jujol in the Architecture Room of the Fine Arts Exhibition of Paris.

1909

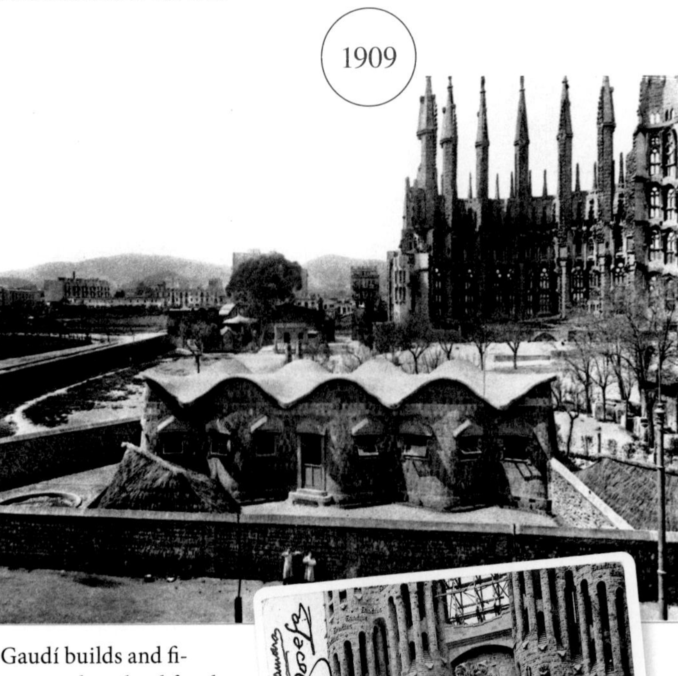

Gaudí builds and finances the school for the children of the Temple workers.

1910

The bell towers reach 62 metres.

1902

A Otto Wagner completes the Post Office Savings building in Vienna.

A Howard presents a new urban planning model: garden cities.

A Méliès premieres *Journey to the Moon,* the first science-fiction film.

A Daniel Burnham builds the "Flatiron" Fuller building in New York.

1903

G Gaudí begins the restoration of the cathedral of Mallorca.

A Lluís Domènech i Montaner builds the Casa Lleó Morera.

A Puig i Cadafalch builds the Casa Terrades (Casa de les Punxes).

1904

G Gaudí begins construction work on the Casa Batlló.

1905

A Fauvism begins with the first exhibition in the Autumn Room in Paris.

A Domènech i Montaner begins the construction of the Palau de la Música Catalana.

A Aristide Maillol sculpts *Mediterranean.*

A Hermann Hesse writes *Beneath the Wheel.*

A Jules Verne dies.

S Albert Einstein forms the theory of relativity.

1906

G Gaudí begins the construction of the Casa Milà.

A Cézanne paints *Mont Sainte-Victoire.*

S Ramon y Cajal wins the Nobel Prize for Medicine.

1907

A Picasso paints *Les Demoiselles d'Avignon.*

1909

H The 26 July to the 2 August marks the Tragic Week in Barcelona with the burning of churches.

1910

A Cubist exhibition on the Salon des Indépendents.

A Delaunay paints *Eiffel Tower.*

1911

H The National Confederation of Workers (CNT) is founded in Spain.

H The Mexican Revolution begins with the movements of Zapata and Madero.

A Frank Lloyd Wright builds his Taliesin home and studio in Spring Green, Wisconsin.

A Salvador Valeri builds the Casa Comalat.

A Krichner paints *Female nude with hat.*

A Braque paints *Man with guitar.*

A Kandinsky publishes *Concerning the Spiritual in Art.*

1913

A Proust publishes *In Search of Lost Time.*

A The word "jazz" is published for the first time.

A Stravinsky premieres *The Rite of Spring.*

1914

H The First World War breaks out.

A Paul Abadie completes the Sacre Coeur in Paris.

1915

A Falla writes the ballet *El Amor Brujo.*

A Eugeni d'Ors publishes *Glossari.*

1911

Drawing by Gaudí of the project for the Passion Façade.

1915

Visit by Nuncio Ragonesi and King Alfonso XIII.

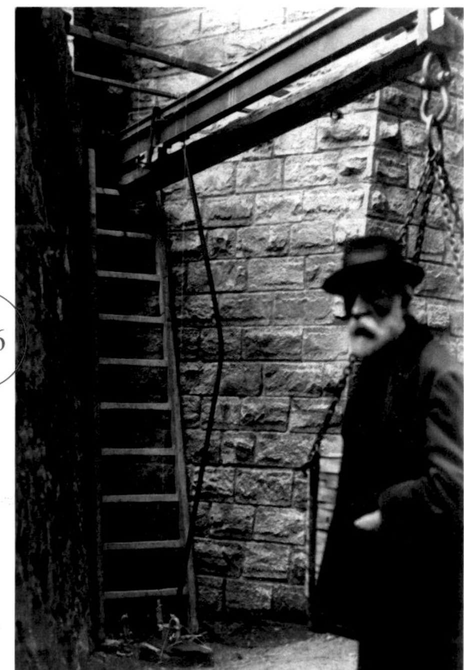

1916

Gaudí supervises a test of resistance of the materials for the construction of the Temple. This year, Gaudí asks for donations from the traders of Barcelona.

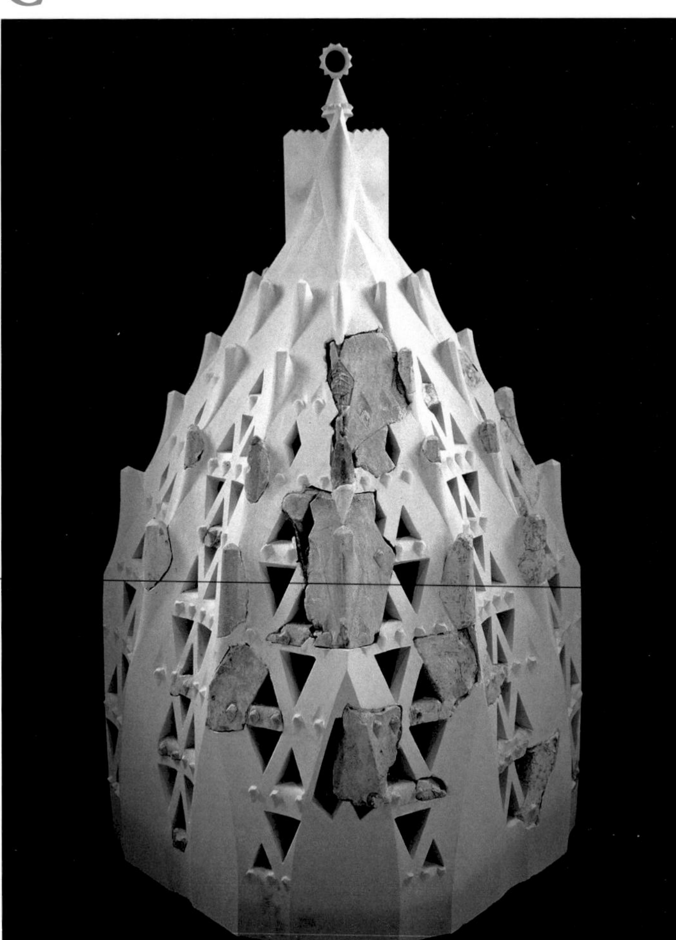

The completed model of the sacristies and the interior study of the columns and vaulting of the Sagrada Família.

1922

1916

A Dadaism emerges in Zurich.

A Freud publishes *Introduction to Psychoanalysis.*

1917

H Russian Revolution: Lenin's Bolshevik Party take power.

1918

H Germany and the allied powers sign an armistice that ends the First World War.

A Josep M. Jujol builds the church of Vistabella in Tarragona.

A First exhibition by Joan Miró.

A Apollinaire publishes *Caligramas.*

1919

H The Treaty of Versailles is signed.

H The Third International is created in Moscow.

A Gropius founds the Bauhaus School in Germany.

A Oskar Kokoschka paints *Double Portrait.*

1920

A Ludwig Mies van der Rohe presents a project for glass

Gaudí's workshop with models of the gargoyles of the apse, the ox of the nativity scene and Saint George from the Casa Botines.

1925

skyscrapers in Berlin.

A Ramón María del Valle-Inclán publishes *Divinas Palabras.*

1921

A Erich Mendelsohn completes the Einstein Tower, close to Potsdam, Germany.

A Pirandello publishes *Six Characters in Search of an Author.*

A Schonberg develops his *Method of composition with 12 sounds.*

1922

H Mussolini takes power in Italy.

A Joyce publishes *Ulysses.*

1923

H Dictatorship of Miguel Primo de Rivera after a coup d'état. It will last until 1930.

A Le Corbusier builds the Maison La Roche.

1924

H Stalin takes political power in the Soviet Union.

A Breton publishes the first *Surrealist Manifesto.*

A Rudolf Steiner builds the Goetheanum.

A Paul Klee paints the *Botanical Theatre.*

A Thomas Mann publishes *The Magic Mountain.*

1925

G Gaudí sees the completion of the Saint Barnabus bell tower (Sagrada Família).

A The Arts Decoratifs Exhibition is held in Paris that hosts the best Art Deco architecture.

A The Bauhaus moves to a building in Dessau, designed by Walter Gropius.

A Dalí paints *Girl at the Window.*

A Dreier premieres *The House Owner.*

1926

S John Logie Baird shows the world how the first TV system works.

Tower of the apostle Barnabus, the only one completed in Gaudí's lifetime.

1925

1926

Gaudí dies after being run down by a tram. The architect was buried in the crypt of the Temple of the Sagrada Família.

Glossary

akashic record It is the large archive of knowledge, experiences and feelings of humanity throughout history, placed everywhere an nowhere.

angelic hierarchies The hierarchy of heavenly bodies is down to the writings of Dionysius the Aeropagite in the 6th century. In this work the angels are divided into three hierarchies each made up of three choirs. In the first hierarchy are Seraphim, Cherubim and Thrones. In the second, Dominions, Virtues and Powers, and in the third, the one most related to humanity, Principalities, Archangels and Angels.

antiphony Brief passage, generally taken from the Holy Scripture, which is sung or said in prayer before and after the psalms and the canticles in the canonical hours, and are related to the daytime mass.

archivolt Series of mouldings that decorate an arch on its vertical exterior face, accompanying the curve in all its extension and terminating in the impost.

avatar In Hinduism it is the earthly incarnation of a deity, by extension the descent or personalisation of all deity.

baldachin Pavilion that covers the altar.

base Body that is placed below the shaft of a column, and which is formed of the base and pedestal.

buttress Stone pillar.

canopy Furnishing at a certain height covering or sheltering an altar, seat of honour, bed, etc., open at the front in the form of a pavilion and falling behind in the form of drapes.

columns J and B According to the Bible, when Solomon built the temple of Jerusalem he had the help of a Phoenician artist (Hiram Abiff) full of wisdom and understanding, who raised two bronze columns at the entrance to the temple. The column on the right (north) he called Jachin and the one on the left (south), Boaz. In Masonic tradition both columns are preserved (although inside the temple) identified by the letters J and B.

crucible Recipient of alchemists, generally of clay, used for the transmutation of raw material.

cresset Piece of iron over which the torches are placed for lighting.

dome base Cylindrical body that serves as the base of the dome and rests immediately over the main arches.

dominical Texts and lessons from the Holy Scriptures that in Catholic services correspond to every Sunday and whose subject matter depends on the liturgical calendar. This calendar is related to the life of Jesus Christ (birth, death and resurrection) and is divided into four main time periods: Advent and nativity (which mark the time prior to the birth of Christ and his birth itself; 6 weeks), Lent and Easter (the time before the Passion of Christ and the passion and death; 5 weeks), Whitsun (the time after the resurrection of Christ and the descent of the Holy Spirit and beginning of the activity of the Church; 7 weeks) and the Ordinary Time (the largest part of the year in which nothing special is celebrated and which takes place between Christmas and Lent and between Whitsun and Advent.

epistle Part of the mass, before the gospel, in which a passage from the canonical epistles is read or sung (the letters that the first apostles, especially Paul, wrote to the Christian communities spread around the Roman Empire).

eucharist In the Catholic Church, a sacrament instituted by Jesus Christ, through which, by the words pronounced by the priest, the bread and wine is transubstantiated into the body and blood of Christ respectively.

faldstool Special seat that bishops use in some pontifical functions.

gnomon Old instrument of astronomy, made up of a vertical needle and a horizontal circle, through which, observing the direction and longitude of the shadow projected by the needle over the circle, the azimuth and height of the sun was determined.

gospel History of the life, doctrine and miracles of Jesus Christ, contained in the four narrations that carry the name of the four evangelists (Matthew, Mark, Luke and John) and which form the first canonical book of the New Testament.

hallelujah Each of the prints that, forming a series, explain an event, generally in rhyming verse.

Jacob's ladder It is a ladder mentioned in the Bible (Genesis 28:11-19), along which the angels ascend and descend to and from Heaven. It was seen by the patriarch Jacob during a dream, after his escape due to his confrontation with Esau.

litany Request to the Virgin (or also to Jesus) with their eulogies and attributes placed in order, which is often sung or said in prayer after the rosary.

lantern Small tower higher than it is wide and with windows, which is placed to crown some buildings and over the semicircular domes of churches.

mandala This word means circle, but it is a composition of abstract geometric forms that help contemplation and concentration.

mullion Architectural piece, long and thin (generally a column that divides a gap, often doors or windows) in two parts vertically.

mysteries of Eleusis Initiation rites that followed the Homeric Hymn dedicated to Demeter and which were held annually in the locality of Eleusis, close to Athens.

pantocrator In Byzantine and Romanesque art, representation of the Saviour seated, blessing and framed in a form of an almond.

paraboloid Surface generated by the movement of a parabola that revolves around its axis of symmetry.

pediment
a) Parapet or low wall built over the entablatures to conceal the height of the roof, and usually decorated with pedestals.
b) Triangular crowning of a façade or portico.

sanctus Part of the mass, after the preface and before the canon, in which the priest says this word three times. In English saint, formerly called Trisagilon for being a hymn in honour of the Holy Trinity, in which 'saint' is repeated three times.

seven sorrows of Saint Joseph
The Catholic tradition commemorates seven moments from the life of Saint Joseph in which he suffered sorrow and divine consolation (joys).
• The sorrow of discovering the pregnancy of his wife, Mary (the joy when the Archangel revealed to him the sublime mystery of incarnation).
"The angel of the Lord appeared to him in his dreams and said to him: Joseph. Son of David, do not fear receiving Mary, your wife, since that conceived within her is the Holy Spirit. She will give birth to a son and you are to give him the name Jesus" (Mathew 1, 20-21).
• The sorrow of seeing the baby Jesus born in poverty (the joy of hearing the harmony of the choir of angels and observing the glory of that night).
• The sorrow when the blood of Jesus was spilt in his circumcision (the joy from giving him the name of Jesus).
"She will give birth to a son, and you are to give him the name Jesus, because he will save his people from their sins" (Mathew 1, 21).
• The sorrow of Saint Joseph with the prophecy of Simeon, on predicting the suffering of Jesus and Mary (the joy at the same time, in the prediction of the salvation and resurrection of the souls).
• The sorrow in his desire to educate and serve the Son of the Almighty, especially on the flight to Egypt (the joy of always having God himself with him, and of witnessing the falling of the idols of Egypt).
"The angel of the Lord appeared to Joseph in a dream and told him: Get up, take the child and his mother and escape to Egypt. Stay there until I tell you, for Herod is going to search for the child to kill him".
(Matthew 2,13).
• The sorrow caused by the fear of Archelous (the joy of returning with Jesus of Egypt to Nazareth and the trust established through the Angel.
"So he got up, took the child and his mother and went to the land of Israel. But when he heard that Archelous was reigning in Judea in place of his father Herod, he was afraid to go there"
(Matthew 2, 21-22).
• The sorrow when guiltless, he loses Jesus, and searched for him anxiously for three days (the joy on finding him amidst the teachers in the Temple).
"They sought him among their relatives and acquaintances. So when they did not find him, they returned to Jerusalem, seeking him" (Luke 2, 44-45).

singing gallery Balcony over the naves of a church where the mass singers would be situated.

Solomonic column A column with the shaft contoured in a spiral.

swirling dervishes Sufís from the school created by Rumi. They are known for the dance consisting of spinning dizzily round and round.

triforium Gallery surrounding the interior of a church over the arches of the naves and which usually has windows of three spaces.

twelve fruits of the holy spirit
Tradition of the Catholic Church numbers twelve perfections that the Holy Spirit works among the faithful as priorities of eternal life. They are: charity, joy, peace, patience, benignity, goodness, long-suffering, mildness, faith, modesty, continency and chastity.

Vedic Of the Vedas or relating to these holy Hindu books. Vedas are the four Sanskrit texts that form the basis of the extensive system of holy scriptures of Hinduism.

ziggurat Temple of Mesopotamian cultures dedicated to observation of the stars. It is a pyramid of 7 terraces, that correspond to the 7 first planets, the 7 basic colours, etc.

Zoroastrianism Religion of a dualist nature, reformed by Zoroaster from an exclusively monotheist interpretation.

[5] Hope Doorway | [4] Charity Doorway | [5] Faith Doorway

7 The two columns
8 Chameleons
9 Tortoises
10 Angels of the Final Judgement
11 Central column
12 The ox and the mule
13 The shepherds of the Adoration
14 Three kings of the Orient
15 Musician angels
16 The star
17 Rosary
18 Annunciation and Incarnation
19 Signs of the Zodiac
20 The Coronation of Mary
21 Name of Jesus
22 Pelican
23 The egg
24 The cypress and the doves
25 The tau, the X and the dove
26 Ladders
27 Bridge
28 Birds
29 Holy Innocents
30 Betrothal of the Virgin Mary
31 Flight to Egypt
32 Wise man and the Child Jesus
33 Trunk saw and other tools
34 Saint Joseph on the boat
35 Group of Jesus preaching, the Workshops in Nazareth and the Visitation
36 Heart of Jesus
37 Presentation of the Child Jesus in the temple
38 The Virgin
39 The lantern of the Holy Trinity
40 Grapes and wheatears
41 Palm leaves
42 The Providence

[1] Nativity Façade

For Rita,
the pearl that came with the spring.

ALBERT FARGAS

Published by
© Triangle Postals SL

Text
© Albert Fargas

Chronology and glossary
Josep Liz, Genís Puig

Photography
© Pere Vivas, Ricard Pla, Biel Puig

Graphic design
Joan Colomer

Layout and photographic retouching
Oleguer Farriol, Biel Puig

Translation
Steve Cedar

Archive photographs
© Junta Constructora del Temple Expiatori
de la Sagrada Família
© Arxiu Mas
© Càtedra Gaudí

Illustrations
© Junta Constructora del Temple Expiatori
de la Sagrada Família
© Dissenys Papeti SL

Acknowledgements
Josep Faulí, Teresa Martínez de Dalmases,
Laia Vinaixa, Etsuro Sotoo,
Museu d'Història de Barcelona (MUHBA)

Printed by
Sanvergràfic

Registration number
B-32564-2009

ISBN
978-84-8478-406-7

Junta Constructora del Temple Expiatori
de la Sagrada Família
Sicília, 286
08013 Barcelona
Tel. 34 93 207 30 31
Fax 34 93 476 10 10
www.sagradafamilia.org
informa@sagradafamilia.org

TRIANGLE POSTALS

Pere Tudurí, 8
07710 Sant Lluís, Menorca
Tel. 34 971 15 04 51
Fax 34 971 15 18 36
www.triangle.cat

[44] Faith Doorway

[43] Charity Doorway

[45] Hope Doorway

46 Last supper
47 Malchu's ear
48 Magic square
49 Betrayal of Judas
50 Flagellation
51 Alpha-Omega

52 Denials of Peter
53 Labyrinth
54 Crown of thorns
55 Jesus before Pontius Pilate
56 Way of the Calvary
57 Veronica

58 Longinus
59 Playing for the robes
60 Crucifixion
61 Sepulchre
62 The burial
63 Ascension of Jesus

[2] The Passion Façade